BRINGING THE WORD TO LIFE

BRINGING THE WORD TO LIFE

Engaging the New Testament
through Performing It

Richard F. Ward *&* David J. Trobisch

William B. Eerdmans Publishing Company
Grand Rapids, Michigan / Cambridge, U.K.

Published 2013 by
Wm. B. Eerdmans Publishing Co.
2140 Oak Industrial Drive N.E., Grand Rapids, Michigan 49505 /
P.O. Box 163, Cambridge CB3 9PU U.K.
www.eerdmans.com

Printed in the United States of America

18 17 16 15 14 13   7 6 5 4 3 2 1

Library of Congress Cataloging-in-Publication Data

Ward, Richard F.
Bringing the Word to life: engaging the New Testament through performing it /
Richard F. Ward & David J. Trobisch.
pages   cm
Includes bibliographical references (pages   ).
ISBN 978-0-8028-6885-5 (pbk.: alk. paper)
1. Bible. N.T. — Criticism, interpretation, etc. 2. Oral tradition —
Religious aspects — History. 3. Oral reading. 4. Storytelling —
Religious aspects — Christianity.   I. Trobisch, David.   II. Title.

BS2361.3.W37   2013
225.6 — dc23

2012043182

Unless otherwise noted, the Scripture quotations in this publication are from the
New Revised Standard Version of the Bible, copyright © 1989 by the Division of
Christian Education of the National Council of Churches of Christ in the U.S.A.,
and used by permission.

Contents

HOW PERFORMANCE CRITICISM INFORMS
THE INTERPRETATION OF THE TEXT

PERFORMANCE TODAY:
FROM PREPARATION TO REVIEW

Contents

Introduction

A Text in Performance (RW)

As a graduate student in the School of Speech at Northwestern University, I was invited to attend a Christmas party in Evanston in the home of one of my advisors, Bob Jewett. He was hosting a party of his colleagues in New Testament who were attending a meeting of the Society of Biblical Literature in Chicago. In the spirit of the season, there were refreshments, and of course there was both hilarity and serious conversation about their shared passion for their teaching and research in biblical studies. There was even some carol-singing around the piano.

At one point in the evening, Dr. Jewett called upon Thomas Boomershine, a professor at the United Theological Seminary in Dayton, Ohio. "The evening wouldn't be complete without a story, Tom," Jewett said. "Do you have one you might tell us?" Tom smiled shyly and said yes. All of us in the room were alert to what story he would tell on such an auspicious occasion. And then, a story unfolded simply and directly, but in a way that captured us all in its web.

It was the story of Jesus' birth as recorded by Luke the Evangelist. Tom was using the very words of a standard translation. How many times had I either read that story for myself or heard it read? And yet I felt as if I was listening to it for the very first time! I looked around at the others in the room. Here were women and men who had made the study of the Christian Bible their life work. All of us in that room had had courses and seminars that established the proximity of New Testament literature to orality. Yet few if any of us knew what else to make of that study except to look for the residue of oral communication in the literary and rhetorical forms present in the New Testament. The story as Tom told it did something else with that knowledge. He turned the text into a form of living speech and held us all in rapt attention, in the stillness and reverent silence that sacred stories can create. The familiar text had come to life all over again in the telling.

What impressed me most was how the words of the text had become more than just a reading; they had established a *presence* that became more than the sum of its parts. Tom wasn't talking *about* the story. He gave no commentary and no explanation of its significance in any way. He was talking *with* the story — that is, his voice and body were conjoined in a relationship to the language, thought, and intentionality of the story as it was. His telling demonstrated not only a deep knowledge of the text but also a command of how the text speaks and a trust that the story, through him, would do its own work in the listeners' hearing of it. Somehow, who Tom Boomershine was, who we were, and what the story spoke of coalesced as an *experience* of the text that we were all sharing. It was as if we were hearing the text for the first time.

The manner of his presentation was also intriguing. It was similar to other modes of performance I was familiar with but didn't quite conform to any one of them. It resembled theatre because Tom treated the biblical text like a "script" and spoke it *as if* he was "acting" the part of the biblical narrator. Yet he wasn't "in character" — he wasn't impersonating a character developed by a playwright. The presentation had the spontaneity of storytelling, but the teller of the story was sticking closely to the words of a text that he himself had not created. It was more like an oral interpretation of a text, except he had internalized the actual text — it was not something that he held in his hands or referred to on a lectern.

Since the text proclaimed "the good news," it sounded a bit like a sermon that is spoken without notes. What I saw and heard was a mixed modality of performance that blurred the boundaries of genre, drawing from other verbal art forms without strictly defining itself as any one of them. It was a form of communication that fit the form, purposes, and intentions of the text.

In seminary I had learned that the Gospel genre in itself was unique. Gospels are more like collections of stories, sayings, remembrances, and commentary stitched together in a narrative whole and intended to make a theological point — that Jesus of Nazareth was sent or chosen by God to assume a primary role in the drama of God's salvation. Boomershine's presentation was a performance that completed the thoughts, intentions, and affect of the text in a way that silent, solitary reading could not. It took us into a place that only performance of a biblical text can — to that fluid, shifting place between writing and speech, that place where the texts like these came from.

One of the things that biblical studies awakens is an interest in "origins," as in "Where did this text come from?" Performing a text awakens an interest in origins too — "How was a text like this *done*?" "How *was* it 'performed'?" And then, "How shall I perform it now?" Asking these questions together brings about a vital collaboration between performance studies and biblical interpretation through the practice of performing literature. Performance study of biblical texts yields new, imaginative ways to experience them and to present the interpreter's understanding of both the texts and the narrative worlds they come from.

Introduction

Listening with the Heart (DT)

In antiquity, literature was almost always read out aloud to an audience. And the Christian Bible is no exception. Readers experienced the text by watching and listening to a performer *doing* the text. Authors designed their works as records of sound bites. And even in the unfortunate case when there was no one available to perform, people would read the text aloud to themselves, experiencing it orally, and not as we often do today, when we read in silence. At the time of Jesus, when passages of the Hebrew Bible were read aloud during worship, interpreters would immediately translate them into Aramaic, the language of the people. The so-called *Targum* was done in an effort to make the text accessible to everyone. Interpreters would sometimes paraphrase and elaborate as they put the sacred reading into the words of the living language, relating the message to the current situation of their audience.

When Paul writes to the Thessalonians, he insists that his letter be read aloud to everyone (1 Thess. 5:27). In 1 Timothy, Paul prepares Timothy for his leadership role in Ephesus by reminding him of three qualities of a good pastor: to teach *(didaskalia)*, to exhort *(paraklēsis)*, and to perform the Scriptures in public *(anagnōsis)* (1 Tim. 4:13).

Richard Ward and I met at Yale Divinity School. He was teaching homiletics; I was teaching New Testament. One of our students had died tragically only a few weeks before her graduation, and we were all in deep shock. Richard was asked to preach at the memorial service, an impossible task. Instead of giving a sermon, Richard performed the story of the raising of Lazarus. He didn't change a word of the biblical text. As academics we are trained to be analytical, to listen with our brains, but that day I listened with my heart and understood. In the face of tragedy, we were speechless. The story of Lazarus — or, to be more precise, Richard's performance of the story — captured it all: pain, helplessness, and hope.

Richard and I became good friends, and we have taught numerous workshops all over the country, encouraging others to learn how to open up the familiar biblical texts in new ways for the people they serve. We wrote this book for those who asked us to write it: pastors, parishioners, academic colleagues, and our students.

The Outline of This Book

In the first part of our book, we want to introduce you to performance theory and practice as they apply to the period when the New Testament writings were conceived, written, collected, published, and first performed. Using the teachings of theorists like Quintilian and the voices of creative writers of the period, Richard will paint a picture of what we know about the Roman-Hellenistic culture of performance in the first and second centuries.

The thread then is picked up by David, who walks the readers through a page of a typical early manuscript of the New Testament and explains what it took to perform such a script in public.

In the second part of our book, David explores the benefits of this approach for academic teaching and advocates performance criticism as a scholarly exegetical method. By recreating the setting for which the texts were designed, the interpreter can experiment with a wide range of possible authorial intentions and experience and document the effect a public reading of a specific text has on an audience.

In the third part of our book, we share our experiences as workshop organizers and provide an outline, examples, and exercises that we found helpful. Our hope is that this section will provide practical suggestions for leading a group through the meaningful exercise of exploring New Testament texts through performance in an academic classroom or in a congregational setting.

For students who want to dig deeper into the academic research concerning the topics addressed, we have included an extended bibliography.

We begin all our classes, rehearsals, and performances with a brief prayer. Here is David's favorite:

Spirit of God,
Open our eyes, so we may see,
Open our ears, so we may hear,
And open our hearts, so we may understand.
AMEN.

PERFORMANCE IN ANTIQUITY

Theory in Practice in Roman-Hellenistic Culture

Quintilian's Instructions on How to Perform

Introduction

On the wall of an ancient Roman villa in Pompeii, Naples, there is a painting depicting a performance. A robed figure is standing, speaking and clasping a scroll in the left hand. The performer's right hand is lowered, loose and at rest; an extended forefinger points to the floor of the stage. The artist has draped a toga across the left arm. The performer's face, unmasked, is a thoughtful countenance, revealing that the piece being presented is no comic diversion; its subject is serious. It seems that we have here a visual record of a genre of communication that the culture valued highly.

What *kind* of performance from the Augustan period are we seeing in this painting? What traditions of oral performance are represented here, and what standards of excellence govern its practice? Is this performer an orator, a singer, or an actor? He is a *solo performer of literature* and is practicing a lively and pervasive form of aesthetic communication in the Hellenistic world of the first century CE. It is certainly a kind of performance that the early Christians in that culture were familiar with. Painted on that wall is a representative of performance tradition that is as old as the development of writing. It presented to the Christians of that era an image of how writings of great importance were communicated.

The *performance of literature* is a verbal art form that has a rich history of practices. It explores questions of meaning by transforming the expressive language found in a text into lively speech, rhythm, and sound. Effective oral performance yields for both the performer and the audience not only a deeper understanding of a text but also the experience shared by means of that text. It is a tradition of "aesthetic" communication, comparable to other forms of public address that are shaped or molded into patterns that appeal to the senses, stir the emotions, and heighten knowledge.[1] A performer of literature may find those patterns in either oral or written traditions of expressions and use them to engage an audience.

Along with other oral communicators of that era, the solo performer of "voicings,"[2] whether oral or written, shaped the various ways that Hellenistic Christians communicated their stories and offered interpretations of their experiences by means of gospels, rites, rituals, and letters. The literary traditions that we have received from these early communities reflect what some of the content of early Christian speech was. Looking at the conventions of literature in performance in their cultural context suggests how those emergent traditions were communicated, what the contexts were for the performances of those texts, and what aesthetic principles guided them. Today we take time to look at these principles because we are not the first to live through and experience an intense transformation in the media we use to communicate what is most important to us.

1. Ronald J. Pelias, *Performance Studies: The Interpretation of Aesthetic Texts* (New York: St. Martin's Press, 1992), p. 19.

2. Walter J. Ong, *Orality and Literacy: The Technologizing of the Word* (London: Routledge, 1982). Ong prefers "voicings" to "literature" to describe oral performances of this sort, preferring to place the accent on the oral rather than the written character of texts (p. 14).

Principles that these ancients used to form and to frame their ideas and practices for communication have endured media transformations, helping to shape the ways our Christian ancestors spoke about what they had experienced through God's revelation in Christ. We have of course adapted and modified the performance traditions of these ancestors but have forgotten much of what they taught us about communicating the texts they composed. Once we see what the social and political realities were in that era and how vibrant the art of the solo performer was in response to those realities, we will see what innovative communicators these early Christians were.

It is difficult for us — shaped as we are by the developments of print, electronic, and now digital media — to imagine the universe of communication that gave rise to Christian Scriptures. It was primarily an *oral* world where the technology of writing served the spoken word and expanded its possibilities for communication. "Literature" in this world was inextricably bound to speech; "reading" was done out loud. Texts were "published" by means of public performances. Poets, historians, and dramatists who hoped to gain recognition and appreciation for their work were dependent upon performance skills of their own or those of a trusted representative.

The solo performer of literature had a significant role to play in the Hellenistic culture because of the nature of the art form and the political realities of the era. Neither oratory nor theatre flourished in the Greco-Roman culture of the first century CE. The transition from the republican form of government to the rise of Augustus had an impact on freedom of expression in Rome. "Although Augustus did not set out to limit freedom of speech or suppress oratory," George Kennedy observes, "his enormous personal power was inhibiting and could not help but affect the conditions of oratory."[3] If

---

3. George Kennedy, *The Art of Rhetoric in the Roman World* (Princeton, N.J.: Princeton University Press, 1972), p. 303.

the rise of the imperial system of government precipitated the decline of eloquence in the empire, the politics of performance in first-century Rome restricted the development of some verbal arts while allowing others to flourish.

A major shift also occurred in sensibilities regarding the theatre in Augustan Rome. In Greek society, the theatre was a centerpiece for religious life. In Rome, the theatre became a disreputable institution. The Roman government of the early empire had a completely different motive for sponsoring performance events than did the Greeks. Religious fervor was not motivation for the events. Instead, the state committed itself to a policy of "bread and circuses" as a palliative for civic abuses.[4] The professional actor was a familiar figure in the imperial culture, but the actor's craft was held in such low regard that no actor could hold citizenship in Rome and continue to act.

Even though acting and oratory declined in this culture, do not assume it was a dark age in the performance history of the West. The performance of literature thrived in this period, taking various forms and demonstrating how this verbal art form could adapt to the political realities of the age. It is ironic that in an era where freedom of expression was suppressed (or at least severely constrained), Romans found ways to publicly confer honors and awards on effective solo performers of literature. There were certainly "stars" in this universe of communication, individual virtuosos who achieved excellence in oral performance.

We have only a few windows left for viewing that universe, and those few that we have are cloudy at best. As tantalizing as it would be to have the big picture to help us with our own understanding of how the early Christians communicated their writings with one other, the big picture is simply not available. Yet there are small windows that can give us a peek. Let's take a look.

4. Vera Roberts, *On Stage: A History of Theatre*, 2nd ed. (New York: Harper, 1962), p. 53.

Quintilian, who was born in Spain and lived from 35 CE to after 96 CE, distinguished himself as one of Rome's most influential teachers of rhetoric. Throughout his career, a parade of students would come before him preparing for careers in politics, the practice of law, and the performance of texts. Quintilian disdained actors but begrudgingly granted them some credit and borrowed from some of their techniques. No doubt his students brought the same questions that would-be performers of texts would ask today. Should I use a manuscript? If so, how should I hold it? What should I wear in performance? What should I do with my hands? With body movement? How do I get my audience to care about the characters in my stories? How can my performance shine a light on what a text means?

You can almost see the teacher trying to hold all these issues in front of him and find some way to address them carefully and clearly, with sensitivity to decorum and also to meaning. I imagine him soliciting the services of a scribe or perhaps a team of scribes and former students to assist him in putting his teaching into writing. Perhaps he even performs and demonstrates what he is saying in the presence of those he trusts to set it down correctly.

What we have from these imagined explorations is a multivolume work attributed to him called the *Institutio Oratoria*. What might Quintilian say to the one who asked, "How do I communicate a text?"

Body Posture and Position

First, Quintilian may have addressed the way the performer was standing before an audience. A good speaker's neck would be straight in order to relax the throat. "Relax your shoulders," he would say. "Don't raise them or contract them." At some point, Quintilian would look into the performer's eyes during the rehearsal to get a clue about the speaker's emotional attitude. "Eyes reveal the tempo of the mind," Quintilian taught, "even without movement."[5] The teacher circled the performer to make sure the performer's weight was evenly distributed over the feet. Quintilian warned against placing either the right foot forward or "straddling the feet when standing still."[6] When the performer did move out of this position, Quintilian instructed that the performer should move diagonally, with eyes fixed on the audience and not averted to the right or the left. This was purposeful movement that helped to keep the listener within the grasp of the text's effect. Movement then as now that is unfocused and without intention (except to alleviate the performer's own anxiety!) pulls unwanted attention to the performer.

Bodily Presence and Appearance

Since Quintilian imagined that the kind of performances he envisioned were to be done only by men, he instructed his students to pay particular attention to their attire; it must be "distinguished and manly," he wrote. The performer would pay particular attention to the cut of his toga, the style of his shoes, and the arrangement of his hair. As he stood, the performer would raise the thumbs of his hands and slightly curve his fingers, unless of course he was holding a manuscript. Manuscripts were simply memory aids. No performer could excel unless he spoke the words in a manner suitable to the thoughts and emotions expressed in the text, as if the words were the performer's own. To do so required that a performer have such "natural" gifts as a good voice, excellent lung capacity, and general good health. Audiences would note that performers of literature were charismatic figures who practiced their

5. Quintilian, *Institutio Oratoria*, trans. H. E. Butler, Loeb Classical Library (Cambridge, Mass.: Harvard University Press, 1920), Book 11, 3: 285.
6. Quintilian, *Institutio Oratoria*, Book 11, 3: 311.

art with wit and charm. Unlike the professional actor, the performer of literature, like the orator, would be known for his good character — it was what lent credibility and authenticity to the effort. "Without good character," Quintilian would declare, "your technique is worthless."[7]

It would be hard to suppress a smile or even a guffaw at the thought of applying Quintilian's teaching on bodily appearance to the biblical performers of today! Quintilian was focused on preparing aristocratic young men for public careers. Performers today focus on "image" but in a different sense. For the most part, a performer of a biblical text wants to appear "natural," that is, to dress casually and not so set apart as were the ideal performers of old. That said, some performers don a robe or dress in black to delineate the performer's self from the "performing self" of the biblical author.

For the most part, beginning performers just want to "be themselves" in performance. Gifted performers of texts give interpretations that do in fact use the resources and attributes of their own personalities. Yet there is something in the performance that is not a performer speaking as himself or herself. A performer is speaking someone else's words, words of a biblical narrative, reflecting the attitudes and perspectives of that narrator toward characters and plot.

Quintilian was giving a nod to the cultural conventions for public speaking as we give a nod to ours today. What was at stake for his students is very like what is at stake for the performer of a biblical text today. Moves, gestures, and actions need to be purposeful, the performer's manner of speaking needs to reflect the emotional values of the text, and the performer's bodily appearance needs to lend authenticity to and show respect for the audience's experience of a text.

7. Quintilian, *Institutio Oratoria,* Book 1, 1: 26-27.

Performance as Understanding

It is through performance that literary works enter the sensorium of the reader/auditor and thus open new horizons for interpretation. Live performed interpretations are done in communities, construed as "audiences." Literature has a "secret power" which is experienced in performance through "rhythm and melody." The structure of a piece "charms the ear" and "stirs the soul" by giving "force and direction to our own thoughts." To excel as a performer of literature, one must have a thorough acquaintance with all types of literature. The performer of biblical texts today does well to know the differences between narrative and epistle, apocalyptic and prophecy, psalm and proverb. The writer (or writers and editors) of biblical texts selected a genre that was best suited for how that writer wanted to address an audience in his or her own absence.[8]

Knowledge of literary conventions and devices acquainted the performer (in the ancient world as now) with the affective power of a text. "Every kind of writing must be studied," Quintilian stated, so that the performer would know how different writers used language, form, and style.[9] Inflection, pace, and emphasis are vocal elements a performer uses to release the connotative power of words. A performer studies various literary forms — orations, dramas, and poetry — to learn the value of arranging ideas into appealing patterns of perception and persuasion; arrangement and structure enable the performer's memory. Style triggers emotional response by opening up the thought world and emotional life of each character in the work being performed.

8. Quintilian, *Institutio Oratoria*, Book 9, 4: 513; Book 9, 4: 511.
9. Quintilian, *Institutio Oratoria*, Book 1, 4: 61-63.

Empathy and the Communication of Emotion

The emotional, affective values of a piece are particularly important to the oral performance of literature. Quintilian gave a lot of credit to the power of an audience to determine if the speaker was being "natural" or if that speaker was striving for affect. What was "natural" was what was truly being experienced in the performance. "The objective," said Quintilian, "is to excite the appropriate feeling in oneself, to have a mental picture of the facts, and to exhibit an emotion that cannot be far from the truth."[10] Quintilian's first principle for communicating emotion was that *the performer moves an audience by first personally experiencing the emotions felt by a character*. A performer is restrained from histrionic display of emotion by the emotional values of the piece being performed. The task of the performer is to *adapt one's own feelings to those expressed by the character in the piece*. Eloquence and effectiveness spring from a performer's ability to awaken emotions in the audience that are appropriate to the text.

In order to experience the effect of a desired emotion, the performer of literature is encouraged to use the imagination to "make those things absent seem to be present before our eyes. It is the (performer) who is sensitive to such impressions who will have the greatest power over the emotions." To awaken pity, for example, "we must imagine that these ills have befallen ourselves"; to arouse empathy, "we must feel (a particular character's) suffering as if it were our own."[11]

Felt emotion shapes the performer's use of the voice and body. "Voice rages as passion strikes the words."[12] Sound and movement are keys to what the performer is experiencing in relation to the text. An audience will be able to determine degrees of sincerity and insincerity by listening to the tone of the performer's voice and by watch-

10. Quintilian, *Institutio Oratoria*, Book 11, 3: 277.
11. Quintilian, *Institutio Oratoria*, Book 6, 2: 435.
12. Quintilian, *Institutio Oratoria*, Book 11, 3: 277.

ing the movement. "For the voice is the index of the mind," observed Quintilian, "and is capable of expressing all varieties of feeling."[13] So is the body. Gesture is adapted to suit the voice, investing the patterns of expressive movement with meaning. What Quintilian stressed was integration between voice and movement; there had to be congruity between *what was said* and *how it was spoken* in the act of performing it; otherwise, thought and meaning would suffer. "If gesture is out of harmony with what is said, words fail to carry conviction."[14]

In Quintilian's world, one could find and imitate "in nature" styles and postures that would appropriately convey emotion. For example, an arm, slightly extended, with shoulders thrown back, and fingers opening as the hand moved forward highlighted the rhythm of "continuous flowing passages."[15] Restraint and timidity were conveyed by slightly hollowing the hand "as if making a vow," moving it to and fro slightly, and swaying the shoulders in unison. For wonder, the performer turned the head upward while pulling the fingers into the palm, "beginning with the little finger first."[16]

To our sensibilities, such gestures and postures would seem exaggerated or artificial. Quintilian's contemporaries, by contrast, would recognize such behavior as appropriate to the performance of oral and literary traditions. The point was to distinguish or "elevate" some kinds of speaking from ordinary, everyday communication. Today we train our eyes to see what is "aesthetic" or enlivening in everyday speech, but for Quintilian's contemporaries, poetry, drama, and oration were "higher" than the vernacular. Quintilian's students would walk away from sessions like this more aware of the potential of language to "elevate" or enliven the human spirit. Shouldn't that be the goal of performers today as it was for the early performers of Christian texts?

13. Quintilian, *Institutio Oratoria*, Book 11, 3: 277.
14. Quintilian, *Institutio Oratoria*, Book 11, 3: 281.
15. Quintilian, *Institutio Oratoria*, Book 11, 3: 289.
16. Quintilian, *Institutio Oratoria*, Book 11, 3: 289.

Understanding the Form

The objective for the performer of literature is to fully understand what he or she hears or reads so that in performance he or she will make allowances for pauses, breath intake, transitions in thought, and beginnings and endings. *Effectiveness in performance means that the performer must speak words "as if" they were the performer's own.* Quintilian taught that the use of a manuscript in performance indicated to the audience that the reciter did not trust his or her memory. A manuscript in the hand also restricted the use of the body in expression. A performer did extensive memory training so that he or she could readily internalize the language and release the body for use in performance. Sadly, the discipline of memorizing a text has over time become a lost art. It is as if a muscle has gone soft from disuse. Extensive memory training is hard to come by in a rapidly evolving digital age. Something that Quintilian took for granted is not the case today. What David and I teach in our classes is precisely the value of memory training for the study of a biblical text. We do so for the same aesthetic reasons that Quintilian did — to enable the performer to explore and then communicate values of a text that are hidden by practices of silent reading and flattened oral communication.

One of the aims of performance of literature has always been to determine the aesthetic value of a piece of writing or oratory. If the performer refrained from allowing personality to eclipse the experience of the literature, then the power of a text was released for both audience and performer. Listen to what Quintilian had to say: "The speaker stimulates us by the animation of his delivery, and kindles the imagination, not by presenting us with an elaborate picture, but by bringing us into actual touch with the things themselves."[17]

17. Quintilian, *Institutio Oràtoria*, Book 10, 1: 11.

Performance of Literature as Distinct from Acting

It seems that performers of literature have asked in every era, "Is this way of communicating most like acting? What's the difference?" Quintilian was careful to delineate the distinctions between "reading" from "acting"; primarily he objected to acting that was bombastic and therefore "unnatural." He used such acting as a negative example of the kinds of excess speakers and performers often fall into. According to Quintilian, acting too often became a display of verbal art and skill; the performance of literature, by contrast, should strive to *conceal* it. One must not, for example, "ape the vices of the drunkard" or "copy the cringing manners of a slave." He was highly suspicious of the actor's effort to "express the emotions of love, avarice, or fear," since he believed they corrupted the mind and led to bad habits of thought and action. Since acting too easily fell prey to "staginess and extravagance of facial expression, gesture, and gait," Quintilian found the actors' gestures and methods of movement unsuitable for the performance of literature and oratory. By avoiding the excesses of the stage, the orator and performer of literature stood to "love the authority which should characterize the man of dignity and virtue."[18] Even today there is deep resistance to "acting" a text from the Bible. Some church audiences equate particular styles and levels of emotional expression with "acting"; others overassociate acting with "mere entertainment." Some appreciate monologues of biblical characters that use words and situations based in biblical situations but not those of the texts themselves. It is still difficult for most church audiences to think it appropriate to "act" the words of the texts themselves.

In spite of his reservations about acting, Quintilian did believe that the actor could serve both the orator and the performer of literature in at least two helpful ways: pronunciation and imperson-

---

18. Quintilian, *Institutio Oratoria*, Book 11, 3: 349.

ation. A good actor spoke clearly and distinctly. The fact that as great an orator as Demosthenes studied with an actor by the name of Andronicus did not escape Quintilian's notice. From the actor the orator learned the principle that each letter had a particular sound that suited it; the natural voice when sufficiently trained was suitable for the requirements of expressive speech. The speaker or performer learned from the actor how to communicate perspective and attitude toward events described through tone of voice.[19]

Apparently the challenges for Quintilian's students were very much like the challenges we face. His emphasis on articulation and restraint in performance is pertinent today. Media speakers — while polished — speak so rapidly that attitude and even perspective can be lost. "Bombast" is the favorite technique of advertisers and some commentators to get attention. At the same time, we are drawn to those with a talent for articulation (without affectation) and expressive speech, just as Quintilian was.

Impersonation of a character was a highly valued rhetorical device. Speakers in all genres were encouraged by their teachers to "display the inner thoughts of adversaries and to introduce conversations between themselves and others." In this manner a speaker could put words into the mouths of other persons, bringing them to theatrical life! "He [the speaker] may even bring down the gods from heaven, raise the dead, or give voice to entire cities and peoples."[20] The best of the actors were able to persuade audiences by freely using speech that was lively and animated. Such qualities deepened and enhanced the affect of a literary text. Performers "add so much to the charm even of the greatest of poets *that the verse moves us far more when heard than when read.*"[21] To "play" a character, the performer would take the character's fortune, social

---

19. Quintilian, *Institutio Oratoria,* Book 1, 11: 183-89.
20. Quintilian, *Institutio Oratoria,* Book 9, 2: 391.
21. Quintilian, *Institutio Oratoria,* Book 9, 2: 391; italics mine.

rank, and achievement into account. Then the performer would communicate these elements by means of suitable gestures and vocal intonations.[22] What the performer sought in a study of the character was a sense of the character's passion. Unless that passion was communicated, the audience would likely yawn with indifference. "Without it [passion, emotion] all else is bare and meager, weak and devoid of charm."[23]

Some characters in biblical texts are skillfully drawn, while others appear simply as functionaries or foils. In either case, their presence in texts is a lively one and presents an opportunity for the biblical interpreter to bring them into clearer focus for study and even pure delight!

Quintilian's Legacy for Performance Studies

Quintilian imagined that a thorough training for the public speaker included understanding the principles and practices by which literature was brought to life by means of voice, gesture, impersonation, and movement. Such principles became foundational to performance of literature in the West. Sociopolitical conditions in Imperial Rome thwarted the emergence of the kind of ideal orator that Quintilian dreamed of. Yet his principles for performing literature became the standards for excellence in the Greco-Roman tradition of recitation in the first century CE. The highly skilled oral reader was the instrument of publication in the culture.

From Quintilian we do get a sense of how performers in the world of the first Christians brought a text to life. We don't finally know if any of the performers of early Christian texts were trained along these lines. However, what we can see from Quintilian's manual is the particular values in communicating texts that were pres-

---

22. Quintilian, *Institutio Oratoria*, Book 3, 8: 503-507.
23. Quintilian, *Institutio Oratoria*, Book 6, 2: 417.

ent in the culture where the fledging churches were embedded. Through the use of a trained imagination, the skillful performer could bring an audience "into actual touch with the things" remembered in oral traditions or recorded in writing. Voice and gesture, the presentation of felt emotional values, and a thorough knowledge of the style and content of a given text were elements of a verbal art that flourished in the world of communications in which the early Hellenistic Christians fashioned their faith. If Quintilian offers performance values, other sources from the ancient world give us examples of the kinds of performances the early Christians might have seen.

Performance from the Authors' Perspective: Pollio, Pliny, Claudius, Nero

If the first century CE was an era of decline in oratory and theatre, it was at the same time a period of opportunity for a Roman poet, dramatist, or historian to develop a reputation through performance. One occasion for the oral performance of literature was a public recitation. In or about 30 BCE, C. Asinius Pollio established public recitation as a cultural convention.[24] In Pollio's day, the author's practice of inviting guests to his home for an evening of reading and discussion was well-established. Pollio organized public recitation as a more formal occasion, giving it the character it possessed in the early empire. He instituted the practice of giving public readings in the libraries of the great temples in Rome, thereby making literature available to wider audiences.

Pliny the Younger (62–ca. 115) attests to this innovation in performance history. In his Epistle I, Pliny records that the Emperor

---

24. Alexander Dalzell, "C. Asinius Pollio and the Early History of Public Recitation at Rome," *Hermathena* 86 (1955): 27.

Claudius heard a recitation from the Palatine hill, the site of the Temple of Apollo. Augustus oversaw the construction of a library in the temple, and presumably Claudius was hearing the performance there. This was certainly not an isolated event! Pliny writes,

> During the whole month of April scarce a day has passed wherein we have not been entertained with the recital of some poem! Though there is little disposition in the public to attend assemblies of this kind, literary pursuits flourish, and men of genius are not discouraged from producing their performances.[25]

Juvenal's record of his experience of the plethora of recitals in his day is stripped of gloss:

> What? Am I to be a listener only all my days? Am I never to get my word in? I, that have been so often bored by the Theseid of the ranting Cordus? Shall this one have spouted to me his comedies, and that one his love ditties, and I be unavenged? . . . Marble halls are forever ringing until the pillars quiver and quake under the continual recitations![26]

Attending recitals like these were considered social obligations among the aristocracy in Imperial Rome. There were so many of them that Pliny and others did not always give their strictest attention! Some would spend their time during the recital

> . . . seated in the antechambers, talking and sending someone in periodically to inquire whether the author has come in, whether he has read the preface, or whether he has finished the piece. Not

25. Pliny, *Letters*, 2 vols., trans. William Melmoth (Cambridge, Mass.: Harvard University Press, 1941), 1:45.

26. *Juvenal and Persius*, trans. G. G. Ramsay, Loeb Classical Library edition (Cambridge, Mass.: Harvard University Press, 1919), p. 3.

'til then, and even then with the utmost deliberation, they just look in, and withdraw again before the end, some by stealth, and others without ceremony.[27]

There were some performers at least who were as interested in the restoration and reformation of literature as they were in building and securing their own reputations. Titinius Capito wins applause from Pliny not only because he performed himself but because he offered his house to others who wished to give recitals.[28]

Writers benefited from the performance of their work. Orality was an important part of a writer's creative process. After revising a composition in private, a writer would read it aloud to two or three trusted friends, expecting their critique and interpretations. Then that writer might choose to perform it in a recital. Pliny notes what his own writing gained from these practices:

> The reciter himself becomes a keener critic of his work, under the diffidence inspired by the audience. He can discover his hearer's sentiments from the air of a countenance, the turn of a head or eye, the motion of a hand, a murmur of applause, or even silence itself; things which plainly enough distinguish their real judgment from the language of civility.[29]

Sometimes writers didn't trust themselves or their abilities to perform their own work. This seemed to be the case with Pliny. In one of his letters to a friend, he asks whether he should use a freedman to perform in his stead: "He will perform, I know, better than I can, provided his fears do not disconcert him, for he is as unpracticed a reader as I am a poet." Pliny goes on to ask for advice

27. Pliny, *Letters*, 1:47.
28. Pliny, *Letters*, 2:123.
29. Pliny, *Letters*, 1:123.

on how he should conduct himself during the performance of his poetry:

> Now the perplexing question is, how shall I behave while he is reading? Shall I sit silent in a fixed and indolent posture or follow him as he pronounces with my eyes, hands, and voice? (A manner which some, as you know, practice!) But I fancy that I have as little a gift for pantomime as for reading.[30]

If the emperors were suspicious of oratory and theatre, they seemed to enjoy literature in performance to the extent that they engaged in this form of popular entertainment themselves. Claudius was known for his affection for oral performance and the ways it extended his power and influence. For example, he instructed that his own compositions — his Etruscan and Carthaginian histories — be read aloud every two years in the museum he had built in Alexandria.[31] Claudius attempted to perform his own work. On one occasion, his attempt became a performer's nightmare:

> He began to write a history in his youth with the encouragement of Titus Livius and the direct help of Sulpicius Flavus. But when he gave his first reading to a large audience, he had difficulty in finishing, since he more than once threw cold water on his own performance. For at the beginning of the reading the breaking down of several benches by a fat man raised a laugh, and even after the disturbance was quieted, Claudius could not keep from recalling the incident and renewing the guffaws.[32]

30. Pliny, *Letters*, 2:257.

31. Eugene Bahn and Margaret L. Bahn, *A History of Oral Interpretation* (Minneapolis: Burgess, 1970), p. 41.

32. Suetonius, *The Lives of the Caesars*, vol. 1, trans. J. C. Rolfe, Loeb Classical Library edition (Cambridge, Mass.: Harvard University Press, 1914), p. 75.

Should any of us be surprised that Claudius, like Pliny, employed someone else to perform his work? "Even while he was emperor," notes Suetonius, "he wrote a good deal and gave constant recitals through a professional reader."[33] Nero, on the other hand, fancied himself to be an expert in the performance of literature. In *Lives of the Caesars,* Suetonius spins Nero's performing career: "Nero often declaimed in public. He read his poems too, not only at home but in the theatre as well, so greatly to the delight of all that a thanksgiving was voted because of his recital."[34]

Not everyone, apparently, "gave thanksgiving" when Nero performed. Nero considered himself to be an expert not only in declamation and the performance of literature but also in singing. During a musical competition for singers (in which Nero performed), he forbade anyone in the audience to leave, even if a member of the audience was in dire circumstances: "And so it was said that some women gave birth to children there, while many who were worn out with listening and applauding, secretly leaped from the wall, since the gates at the entrance were closed, or feigned death and were carried out as if for burial."[35]

The jealous Nero was capable of bribing, even murdering his rivals. Though he arranged to win the contests he entered, he meticulously followed the rules for competition and rigorously trained for them. Nero's regimen gives a picture of how other performers might have prepared for these events:

He [Nero] was diligent, conscientious, and painstaking in his efforts to perfect his art. Night after night he would listen to Lepinius, the lyre-player; to improve his voice he would forgo fine foods and would lie with a leaden plate on his chest, his

33. Suetonius, *The Lives of the Caesars,* vol. 1, p. 75.
34. Suetonius, *The Lives of the Caesars,* vol. 2, trans. J. C. Rolfe, Loeb Classical Library edition (Cambridge, Mass.: Harvard University Press, 1930), p. 101.
35. Suetonius, *The Lives of the Caesars,* vol. 2, p. 123.

teacher at his side, assiduously practicing vocal exercises. To save his voice, he never addressed his soldiers in person.[36]

Performance of Tragedy in Imperial Rome

Some books of the New Testament — for example, the Revelation of John — can be read as scripts for elaborate dramas, using different voices and a choir. Whether or not tragedies were given the scale of production they were given in classical Greece is contested in performance history. It is likely that political conditions discouraged that genre of performance, especially those pieces that bore anti-imperialistic themes and claims. There was also strong resistance to the spectacular "paraphernalia" the Greeks had used to stage their elaborate tragedies. Whether the resistance was political or aesthetic or both, "tragedy" came to mean something quite different in the performance history of Imperial Rome than it had in Greece. "Tragedy" as it was used by the Romans refers to a number of things: "the ballet of the pantomime artist," performing excerpts from longer, written works, the solo performance of a speech to the accompaniment of a lyre, or the oral recitation of a piece by a single performer or small group of performers of literature. In those cases where an entire work was performed, it was most likely done by a performer who sang/spoke the language of a text as pantomime artists enacted appropriate gestures.[37]

Lucian, a witness to performance of tragedy in this period, observed dancers miming actions while a performer uttered the words of a text.[38] The performer of a piece like this wore a robe, elevated

36. Bahn and Bahn, *A History of Oral Interpretation,* p. 43.

37. H. A. Kelly, "Tragedy and the Performance of Tragedy in Late Roman Antiquity," *Traditio: Studies in Ancient and Medieval Thought, History, and Religion* 35 (1979): 22.

38. Kelly, "Tragedy and the Performance of Tragedy in Late Roman Antiquity," p. 23.

shoes, and used masks. Like their counterparts in ancient Greece, performers would accompany themselves on lyres *(citharoedes)* or act out roles, sing arias, or make use of props and dialogue with other performers *(tragoedeus)*. Sometimes a single performer would play different roles. Lucian gives the following account of an encounter between a solo performer of tragedy and a "foreigner" just before a performance:

> Seeing five masks laid ready — that being the number of parts in the piece — he (the "foreigner") asked who would play the other parts. He was informed that the whole piece would be performed by a single actor. "Your humble servant, sir," cries our foreigner to the artist: "I observe that you have but one body: it had escaped me that you possessed several souls."[39]

St. Augustine notes in his *Confessions* that he performed the literature of tragedy. He coveted the "applause of an audience, prizes for (spoken) poetry, and quickly fading wreaths won in competition."[40] Augustine's love of the art led him to "enter a competition for reciting dramatic verse," but he was repelled by "a sorcerer sent to ask me how much I would pay him to make certain that I won."[41]

Performance of Literature in the Early Church

Obviously, the culture that cradled the fledgling Christian communities had an appetite for performing literature. Effective performers reflected the dominant aesthetic principles: recitative impersonation and creation of the inner lives of characters, emotional

39. Quoted in A. M. Nagler, *A Source Book in Theatrical History* (New York: Dover, 1952), p. 29.

40. St. Augustine, *Confessions,* translated and with an introduction by R. S. Pine-Coffin (New York: Penguin, 1961), p. 71.

41. St. Augustine, *Confessions,* p. 72.

expression, and the capacity to create empathy among the audience were highly valued elements in performance. When Christians came together, they probably expected the same from their performers when they "did" literature generated by memories of Jesus' life and ministry, apostolic letters, wisdom writings, and prophecy, and of course the sacred writings of the Hebrews.

Several texts in the Hebrew Scriptures reveal the centrality of literature in performance to the formation of the Hebrews' religious and cultural identity; these performance conventions were one influence on the practice of reading Scripture aloud in Christian communities. The first explicit textual record of literature in performance is in 2 Kings 23:2. In the eighteenth year of the reign of King Josiah (dated 621 BCE), the book of Deuteronomy was discovered in the Temple by Hilkiah, the high priest, and was given to Shaphan, Josiah's secretary. Josiah heard it read aloud, then ordered it to be read aloud to the people:

> Then the king directed that all the elders of Judah and Jerusalem should be gathered to him. The king went up to the house of the LORD, and with him went all the people of Judah, all the inhabitants of Jerusalem, the priests, the prophets, and all the people, both small and great; he read in their hearing all the words of the book of the covenant that had been found in the house of the LORD. The king stood by the pillar and made a covenant before the LORD, to follow the LORD, keeping his commandments, his decrees, and his statutes, with all his heart and all his soul, to perform the words of this covenant that were written in this book. All the people joined in the covenant. (2 Kings 23:1-3)

Reading aloud in the Hebrew communities of faith had not only aesthetic but also theological and political implications. For example, the text indicates that the public performance of the book of Deuteronomy was part of a strategy to centralize the worship of Yahweh in Jerusalem and to forbid the worship of all other gods.[42]

Here is another example of the political meaning of texts in performance. In 605 BCE, Jeremiah dictated and Baruch wrote a scroll that recorded, as the Lord had instructed Jeremiah, "all the words that I have spoken to you against Israel and Judah and all the nations, from the day I spoke to you, from the days of Josiah until today" (Jer. 36:2). Baruch's scroll provoked the wrath of King Jehoiakim, who heard Jehudi read it:

> . . . And Jehudi read it to the king and all the officials who stood beside the king. Now the king was sitting in his winter apartment (it was the ninth month), and there was a fire burning in the brazier before him. As Jehudi read three or four columns, the king would cut them off with a penknife and throw them into the fire in the brazier, until the entire scroll was consumed in the fire that was in the brazier. (Jer. 36:21-23)

King Jehoiakim's violent response demonstrated resistance not only to the words of the prophet but also to the form in which they were cast. Literature in performance is a contested phenomenon; it privileges some voices while silencing others. While performances of literature can provoke opposition, they can also be instrumental in the formulation of religious identity. Following the destruction of Jerusalem and a long period of exile, the public performance of a text was part of a ritual commemoration of the rebuilding of Jerusalem:

> When the seventh month came — the people of Israel being settled in their towns — all the people gathered together into the square before the Water Gate. They told the scribe Ezra to bring the book of the law of Moses, which the LORD had given to Israel.

42. Thomas E. Boomershine, "Biblical Storytelling," unpublished manuscript, 1985, p. 42.

Accordingly the priest Ezra brought the law before the assembly, both men and women and all who could hear with understanding. This was on the first day of the seventh month. He read from it facing the square before the Water Gate from early morning until midday in the presence of the men and the women and those who could understand. . . . (Neh. 8:1-3)

These vignettes taken from the performance history of Israel form one piece of the backdrop for an analysis of the importance of oral performance of texts in the emerging Christian community. Services of worship were organized for the public reading and oral interpretation of scriptures. The Gospel of Luke records one particular episode that links the performance of literature in Jewish worship with that of the church. To inaugurate his public ministry, Jesus performed and interpreted a sacred text:

When he came to Nazareth, where he had been brought up, he went to the synagogue on the sabbath day, as was his custom. He stood up to read, and the scroll of the prophet Isaiah was given to him. He unrolled the scroll and found the place where it was written, "The Spirit of the Lord is upon me, because he has anointed me to bring good news to the poor. He has sent me to proclaim release to the captives and recovery of sight to the blind, to let the oppressed go free, to proclaim the year of the Lord's favor." And he rolled up the scroll, gave it back to the attendant, and sat down. The eyes of all in the synagogue were fixed on him. Then he began to say to them, "Today this scripture has been fulfilled in your hearing." All spoke well of him and were amazed at the gracious words that came from his mouth. (Luke 4:16-22a)

The Gospel genre arose out of the interface between traditions surrounding Jesus' ministry and their oral interpretations. In his description of the Christian worship in his time, Justin Martyr (c. 103-165) wrote in his First Apology, "The Memoirs of the Apostles or the writings of the Prophets are read as long as time allows. After the reader has finished, the presiding officer verbally instructs and exhorts us to imitate these shining examples."[43]

Eusebius of Caesarea (c. 263-339), reflecting the practices of his time, imagined that those who heard Peter's performances "were not satisfied with a single hearing or with the unwritten teaching of the divine proclamation," so they "besought Mark, whose Gospel is extant, seeing that he was Peter's follower, to leave them a written statement of the teaching given them verbally."[44]

Though this account of Marcan authorship is contested, it does describe an ancient perception of the relationship between orality and literacy in the formation of early Christian Gospel traditions. Performance of these oral traditions may have been "less inhibited than today" and more animated and emotionally expressive.[45] Knowledge of the performance history in this period expands our imaginings of how the early Christians might have experienced their Gospels.

But Gospels were not the only form of literature performed in early Christian communities. The apostle Paul certainly intended that his letters to the communities be read aloud. He freely used formulae borrowed from liturgical performance to open and close his letters. At the end of 1 Thessalonians (5:27) and Colossians (4:16) there are explicit instructions to read the letters aloud and circulate them among other communities. The Pauline author of 1 Timothy instructs the recipient of the letter to read to the people until the apostle arrives (4:13).

---

43. Quoted in Herbert A. Musurillo, S.J., *The Fathers of the Primitive Church* (New York and Toronto: The New American Library, 1966), p. 134.

44. Quoted in Boomershine, "Biblical Storytelling," p. 34.

45. Amos N. Wilder, *Early Christian Rhetoric: The Language of the Gospel* (Cambridge, Mass.: Harvard University Press, 1971), p. 68.

Those who performed New Testament literature had to have particular knowledge and skill in the art of transforming inscription into speech and sound. Since the texts of ancient manuscripts had no punctuation and no spacing, the reader had to supply the divisions of words and sentences from memory. In Hebrew manuscripts there were no markings of vowels. In order to read aloud (as Jesus did in Luke 4:16-21), it was necessary to memorize the vowels.[46] Reading a text aloud for edification and instruction was consistent with the established performance practices of Judaism: "O keen scholar," one rabbi admonishes another, "open your mouth and read (the written tradition), open your mouth and repeat (the oral tradition) so that (your knowledge) may be maintained in you and that which you have learned may live."[47]

Performance of Literature in the City of Corinth

Those who performed apostolic correspondence or Gospels in the Corinthian house churches did so against a rich backdrop of performance history. Corinthians had for centuries sponsored the Isthmian Games, one of the four most important festivals in the Pan-Hellenic world. Dating from the late sixth century BCE, the games were held every two years at a site not ten miles from the city. Though the games were not as greatly regarded as those at Delphi or Nemea, they were popular enough to attract throngs of competitors, spectators, and merchants. Athletes, musicians, poets, performers of literature, and playwrights came from all over Asia Minor and Greece to compete for top awards and prestige at these games.

The president of the games *(agonothetēs)* during the formation of the Corinthian church was L. Castricus Regulus, a chief magis-

---

46. Boomershine, "Biblical Storytelling," p. 47.
47. Quoted in Boomershine, "Biblical Storytelling," p. 47.

trate of the city. Elected by the city council of Corinth, a president was given the responsibility of administering the games, deciding which competitions would be offered, and finding housing for the competitors. The prestigious appointment came with the expectation that the *agonothetēs* would make a substantial contribution toward the expenses of the festival. In fact, presidents of the games often bore the entire financial burden for the event! Regulus's presidency was notable. An inscription praises him for restoring many of the facilities that had fallen into ruin and for giving an elaborate banquet for the Corinthians at the time of the festival.[48]

Paul's visits to the city of Corinth took place during a resurgence of interest in the games. Archaeological evidence indicates that the stadium where the games were held was newly restored during the Pauline period.[49] A racetrack nearby remains in nearly perfect condition! If the quality of the facilities is any indication, then we can be sure that the Isthmian Games attracted top performers in sports and the speech arts.

Competition in the performance of literature was a significant feature of the games. In addition to athletic competition, Regulus instituted poetry contests in honor of the divine Julia Augusta.[50] In the voice of the Cynic philosopher Diogenes, Dio Chrysostom satirized those who competed in the oral arts, placing them in the questionable company of magicians, soothsayers, and lawyers!

> At that time you could hear in the area around the Temple of Poseidon any number of luckless sophists shouting and abusing each other, and their notorious students wrangling among themselves, and many authors reciting their silly compositions,

48. John Harvey Kent, *Corinth, VIII/3: The Inscriptions, 1926-1950* (Princeton, N.J.: American School of Classical Studies at Athens, 1966), p. 70.

49. Jerome Murphy-O'Connor, *St. Paul's Corinth: Texts and Archaeology* (Wilmington, Del.: Glazier, 1983), p. 12.

50. Kent, *Corinth, VIII/3: The Inscriptions, 1926-1950*, pp. 72-73.

poets declaiming their verses to the applause of their colleagues, magicians showing off their marvels, soothsayers interpreting omens, tens of thousands of lawyers twisting lawsuits, and no small number of hucksters peddling whatever goods each one of them happened to have for sale![51]

Even Nero joined the company of competitors at Corinth. In 66-67 CE, he came to Corinth to make a speech, to break ground for a new canal, and to compete for prizes in the performance of literature and musical composition. As was his custom, Nero arranged to bribe the other competitors so that his victory would be assured. One of them, a man named Epirus, refused to withdraw from the competition unless he was given the sum of ten talents. Unwilling to pay that much, Nero sent his henchmen to beat Epirus to the point that he was physically unable to compete. After Nero won the competition, he performed his speech — a proclamation of freedom for the Corinthians.[52]

Others are mentioned in various inscriptions for their excellence in oral performance. Lucius Vivious Florus of Patrus and Corinth was remembered as a "boy singer" who won several contests. Publius Aelius Sospinus, Lucius Marcius Fautinus, Marcus Valerius Tourinius, Peducauis Cestinanus, and Poeseidaius all won renown as performers at the Isthmian Games.[53]

There is another name that surfaces in the performance history of this period, not because of his abilities in oral performance but because of his patronage of the oral arts. An inscription remembers a Corinthian named Erastus who made a substantial contribution to the renovation of the theatre at Corinth in the Pauline era.[54] A freedman who had acquired great wealth in a booming Corinthian

51. Dio Chrysostom of Prusa, "Concerning Virtue," Discourse VIII.
52. Suetonius, *The Lives of the Caesars*, vol. 2, pp. 23-24.
53. Kent, *Corinth, VIII/3: The Inscriptions, 1926-1950*, p. 245.
54. Murphy-O'Connor, *St. Paul's Corinth*, p. 37.

economy, Erastus was a civic official (an *aedile*) who financed the building of a road up to the theatre. In his letter to the Romans, Paul sends a greeting on behalf of a Corinthian civic official by the name of Erastus (Rom. 16:23). Could this be the same Erastus? The scholarship isn't conclusive, but the coincidence is tantalizing. It lends support to the hunch that the Corinthians whom Paul worked with to establish a community of Christ at Corinth were certainly aware of, and quite possibly invested in, the practice of the speech arts at the Isthmian Games. They had a strong appetite for and a high appreciation of excellence in oral performance. Prosperity, newly restored facilities, and strong support for the performance of literature, theatre, music, and other arts attracted the best performers to their area. The strong possibility that Erastus was an acquaintance of Paul's and that he was a member of the church Paul founded at Corinth further strengthens the connection between the church and the performance history of the period.

"The pagan festivals may have been a determining factor in Paul's plan to visit Greece," suggests Oscar Broneer.[55] If that is so, there is a note of irony here. Paul comes into a population which appreciates prowess in the speech arts. Yet he arrives at Corinth vowing "not to use lofty words but to speak simply" (1 Cor. 2:2), acknowledging that he steps into a highly competitive arena where skill in oral discourse is prized as a virtue and linked to assessments of character.

The Role of the Audience

Expressive renditions of cherished oral traditions prompted a wide range of emotional responses from listeners. The narrator could ex-

55. Oscar Broneer, "The Apostle Paul and the Isthmian Games," *Biblical Archaeologist* 25 (1962): 2.

pect them to become involved in the performance of the story, even contesting it at points. Audiences might sing along or audibly quarrel with the teller, hum or harrumph, or perhaps accompany performers with musical instrumentation. Performances of the Jesus traditions forged the core narratives we now call "Gospels." "Gospels" were oral epics, created anew in each performance out of responses to and by listeners, that used established story lines for composition, and that answered theological questions that nagged members of the communities.

Gospels might also have been performed in the same ways as "concert" or "closet" dramas — that is, pieces written as literary exercises or for performance in private homes. In a politically repressive environment like Imperial Rome, the "closet" drama provided the means for a writer to get a hearing from a trusted audience for poetry, moral instruction and philosophy, or political views. The Roman tragedian Seneca is an example of a writer who composed pieces that were

> intended for reading or recital at private gatherings and could never have appeared in what we should call public performance; partly because in many of their scenes the implied condemnation of autocracy would have had too dangerous a topical application and partly because there were, so far as we know, no public opportunities for such performances.[56]

"Closet" dramas were performed either by solo performers or small ensembles. This innovation would provide a compelling model for a Christian writer who looked for ways to express controversial views about the meaning of Jesus' ministry; it allowed the composer of the Gospel to employ literary elements that others would recognize. Gilbert Bilizekian establishes a plausible case that tragedy, in ac-

56. E. F. Watling, Introduction, in Seneca, *Four Tragedies and Octavia*, trans. E. F. Watling (Middlesex: Penguin Press, 1966), p. 17.

cordance with the conventions of the "closet" drama, was a significant influence on the composition of the Gospel of Mark:

> The Gospel of Mark could be the product of the skillful combination of elements as disparate as the evangelical narrative on the one hand, and on the other, compatible literary devices borrowed piecemeal from an established classical paradigm, specifically that of Greek tragedy.[57]

A performer of Mark's Gospel, in accord with the practices of his day, might have recited the Gospel in the privacy of a home or a Christian house church, or in a private hall. While it is unlikely, it cannot be entirely ruled out that a performer may have occasionally used an odeum, or theatre. He or she might have recited while a pantomime artist danced the action of the tragedy, using several masks to delineate the characters. Or he or she might have recited to the accompaniment of flutes, pipes, or cymbals.

The study of the performance traditions and values within the culture that surrounded the earliest Christian communities expands our understanding of how Christians communicated their experience of God in Christ to each other. They developed distinctive ways of putting that experience into words, using the conventions of public speaking that were available to them. There was urgency in this effort then just as there is today — to speak in ways that are comprehensible both to each other and to the culture at large. Their creativity and interpretive insights guide our own expression of our study of these texts.

57. Gilbert Bilezikian, *The Liberated Gospel: A Comparison of the Gospel of Mark and Greek Tragedy* (Grand Rapids: Baker, 1977), p. 16.

Reading an Ancient Manuscript
of the New Testament

At the end of the First Letter to the Thessalonians, Paul salutes the recipients with the words, "Greet all the brothers and sisters with a holy kiss," and he ends the letter with his usual wish, "The grace of our Lord Jesus Christ be with you." But between the greetings and the wish of grace he adds, "I solemnly command you by the Lord that this letter be read to all of them" (1 Thess. 5:26-28).

When Paul asked a congregation to read his letter to everyone, what kind of script did he provide? What did early Christians use when they read texts during their worship services? Although we don't have the original letter Paul sent, we do have a good sense of what texts written to be performed before an audience looked like.

Before the printing press was invented, every book had to be copied by hand. About 5,600 handwritten copies containing New Testament texts have survived to this day.

Scriptio Continua

The oldest manuscripts of the New Testament provide the text in an unstructured format, as the example on page 35 shows. Commas, periods, colons, question marks, and quotation marks are curiously

Papyrus 46, ca. 200. 2 Corinthians 11:33–12:9

University of Michigan Papyrus Collection

absent. No paragraph breaks the flow; no spaces separate the words. The text body looks like a single, long word. Chapter numbers are not part of the manuscript tradition in antiquity, and when they were added to medieval manuscripts, they varied from manuscript to manuscript. The advent of printed editions in the sixteenth century made it possible to standardize chapters and introduce verse numbers.[1]

1. David Trobisch, "Structural Markers in New Testament Manuscripts with Special Attention to Observations in Codex Boernerianus (G 012) and Papyrus 46 of the Letters of Paul," *Pericope: Scripture as Written and Read in Antiquity,* vol. 5:

In antiquity, performers of such texts had to make some of the same decisions that translators into modern languages have to make as they prepare their text for publication: they had to break up the flow of letters, the so-called *scriptio continua,* into words, clauses, sentences, and paragraphs. They had to discern titles, editorial additions, summaries, and other structural signals included in the body of text. They had to use their best judgment to identify unmarked notes and comments added by earlier editors. (Some translators, for example, put editorial comments that are part of the biblical text in parentheses like this.)

Nomina Sacra

In addition to having to structure the continuous flow of letters, performers of the Greek New Testament were confronted with the so-called *nomina sacra,* a system of contractions that had to be interpreted during the oral performance. These words are marked with a line over the letters, and only the first one or two characters and the last one or two characters of the word are written out. ΙΗΣΟΥΣ, for example, is rendered $\overline{\text{ΙΣ}}$, using only the first and the last letter. The words *Christ, Lord, God,* and *Jesus* are almost always marked in this way; other words like *father* (reflecting that this could be a reference to God), *son* (reflecting "son of God" as a reference to Christ), *Jerusalem* (the celestial city), *heaven* (where God resides), and as many as thirty other words are noted often but not always as *nomina sacra.*[2]

Layout Markers in Biblical Manuscripts and Ugaritic Tablets, ed. Marjo C. A. Korpel and Josef M. Oesch (Assen: Koninklijke van Gorcum, 2005), pp. 177-90.

2. A. H. R. E. Paap, *Nomina Sacra in the Greek Papyri of the First Five Centuries* A.D. (Leiden: Brill, 1959). Cf. David Trobisch, *The First Edition of the New Testament* (Oxford: Oxford University Press, 2000), pp. 11-13; Larry W. Hurtado, *The Earliest Christian Artifacts: Manuscripts and Christian Origins* (Grand Rapids: Wm. B. Eerdmans, 2006).

This system is unparalleled in non-Christian literature of the period. The origins are obscure, and the phenomenon continues to pose unanswered questions to the scholarly community. Nevertheless, it is clear that performers were expected to decode the contractions as they read aloud to an audience.

For example, lines 4 and 5 of the text in the image of Papyrus 46 — this is text from 2 Corinthians 12:1-2 — is written this way:[3]

ΕΙΣΟΠΤΑΣΙΑΣΚΑΙΑΠΟΚΑΛΥΨΕΙΣΚ̅Υ̅ΟΙΔΑ
ΑΝΘΡΩΠΟΝΕΝΧ̅Ω̅ΠΡΟΕΤΩΝΔΕΚΑΤΕΣΣΑΡΩΝ

Before someone can read the passage fluently, spaces, breathing marks, and punctuation have to be added, and the *nomina sacra* have to be decoded:

εἰς ὀπτασίας καὶ ἀποκαλύψεις κυρίου. οἶδα
ἄνθρωπον ἐν Χριστῷ πρὸ ἐτῶν δεκατεσσάρων

To imagine the challenges a performer faced, try reading the following English text out loud. Like the oldest copies of the New Testament, it is written in capital letters with spaces and punctuation removed and typical *nomina sacra* contracted:

PAULASERVANTOFJSCHTCALLEDTOBEANAPOSTLESETAP
ARTFORTHEGOSPELOFGDWHICHHEPROMISEDBEFORE
HANDTHROUGHHISPROPHETSINTHEHOLYSCRIPTURES

3. *The Chester Beatty Biblical Papyri: Descriptions and Texts of Twelve Manuscripts on Papyrus of the Greek Bible*, ed. F. G. Kenyon, Fasciculus III supplement: Pauline Epistles (London: Emery Walker Ltd., 1936-37).

THEGOSPELCONCERNINGHIS̄SNWHOWASDESCENDEDF
ROMD̄DACCORDINGTOTHEFLESH

Breaking up the continuous flow of letters into words requires an interpretative decision. The sequence "PAULASERVANTOFJSCHT" can be read as "Paula, servant of Jesus Christ" or as "Paul, a servant of Jesus Christ" — the context will decide. Although it isn't too difficult to understand the text at first reading, it is almost impossible to read an unfamiliar text aloud in a way that an audience can follow.

Today we perceive printed text as visual information — dark spots on a light background — to be decoded quietly. In antiquity, however, literature was designed by its authors to be read out loud. Just like sheet music today, ancient manuscripts were seen as media that preserved sound and required a performer to study them before they could be presented in a meaningful way.

The following examples from modern translations demonstrate how modern editors struggle with some of the same challenges a performer of literature in antiquity would have faced.

Editorial Asides

In John 1:38-39, a short dialogue between Jesus and his disciples is interrupted by an editorial comment:

> When Jesus turned and saw them following, he said to them, "What are you looking for?" They said to him, "Rabbi" (which translated means Teacher), "where are you staying?" He said to them, "Come and see."

The narrator steps out of the story and, addressing his Greek-speaking audience directly, explains that the word *Rabbi* is best translated into Greek as "teacher." A skilled performer might turn slightly and face the audience directly as he delivers the explanation, then return to his original posture to continue the dialogue in the narrative world of the story. The Gospel according to John is full of such asides. The editors of the NRSV chose to put them between parentheses.

Differences in Sentence Structure

When verse numbers were added to printed editions of the Greek text in the sixteenth century, the publisher structured 1 Corinthians 14:32-34 the following way:

32 And the spirits of the prophets are subject to the prophets.

33 For God is a God not of disorder but of peace as in all the churches of the saints.

34 Women should be silent in the churches. For they are not permitted to speak, but should be subordinate as the law also says.

The phrase "as in all the churches of the saints" is connected to the previous sentence, underlining that God is a God of peace everywhere. "Women should be silent in the churches" forms a new sentence. The King James Version followed the Greek edition. However, the translators of the Revised Standard Version (1946) structured the passage differently:

32 And the spirits of prophets are subject to prophets. 33 For God is not a God of confusion but of peace. // As in all the churches of the saints, 34 the women should be silent in the churches. For they are not permitted to speak, but should be subordinate as even the law says.

The phrase "as in all the churches of the saints" is attached to the following sentence and seems to give more weight to Paul's statement that women should be quiet. Is this a reflection of the mid-twentieth-century translators' attitude toward the ordination of women, a debate that raged for decades among the Protestant denominations for whom this translation was prepared?

The New Revised Standard Version (1989) goes to great lengths to provide a gender-inclusive translation of the Christian Bible. The editors follow the Revised Standard Version as far as the structuring is concerned, but they put the passage concerning the women in parentheses:

> 32 And the spirits of the prophets are subject to the prophets, 33 for God is a God not of disorder but of peace. // (As in all the churches of the saints, 34 women should be silent in the churches. For they are not permitted to speak, but should be subordinate as the law also says.)

The editors probably did this to support the widely held exegetical theory that these sentences were not written by Paul but added by an early editor. Or do the parentheses also reflect the fact that most Protestant denominations were ordaining women by the time the NRSV was edited? Whatever the reasoning behind the different translations, this example demonstrates how the relevance of a passage shifts simply by adding grammatical marks to a text.

The Illiterate Reader

An interesting document dated February 5 in 304 CE describes a certain Aurelius Ammonius, the lector of a Christian congregation, sending an official letter to the authorities. He declares that the church owned no property except a few bronze objects.[4] Although the lector is obviously the person who performed the Scriptures during the worship services, he had to ask a brother, Aurelius Serenus, to sign the letter. The lector himself was illiterate.[5]

At first, an illiterate or blind performer sounds perplexing. But consider this: Quintilian, the famous Roman teacher of rhetoric and contemporary of Paul, required students to memorize classic speeches "and declaim them standing in the manner which actual pleading required: thus he [would] simultaneously train delivery, voice, and memory."[6] Holding a manuscript would not allow the performer to imitate the body language of the public speaker. Once we understand that ancient manuscripts could be performed only after intensive preparation, which almost certainly included an effort to memorize the manuscript, the notion of illiterate or blind performers makes sense. A good memory becomes more important than literacy or even eyesight. Just as a blind person can be a great musician, a person who cannot read can still be an excellent performer.

Another glimpse into the life of the early church is provided in 1 Timothy. Paul prepares Timothy for his leadership role in Ephesus by reminding him of three qualities of a good pastor: "Until I arrive, give attention to the public reading (ἀνάγνωσις), to exhorting, to teaching" (4:13). It is not teaching or counseling but rather the quality of the performance of literature which is mentioned first.

Our discussion so far indicates that in antiquity reading a New Testament manuscript to an audience required preparation. At a minimum, the *scriptio continua* had to be structured and the

---

4. P. Oxy. XXXIII 2673.

5. The expression in the autographic subscription is μὴ εἰ(δότος) γρά(μματα). For a critical discussion, see G. W. Clarke, "An Illiterate Lector," *Zeitschrift für Papyrologie und Epigraphik* 57 (1984): 106-22.

6. Quintilian, *Institutio Oratoria*, 1.11.14, trans. H. E. Butler (Cambridge, Mass.: Harvard University Press, 1920; rpt. 1996, LCL 124), p. 189.

nomina sacra had to be decoded before a text could be performed. It is also clear that excellent performances of literature were done from memory.

The Reading Context: Early Christian Sanctuaries

At the time when the New Testament writings originated, Christians met in private homes or — like other Hellenistic cult groups — rented rooms in restaurants for their meetings. First Corinthians documents that the meetings of the "church of God in Corinth" (1 Cor. 1:2) were organized around a full meal (1 Cor. 11:21). A certain Gaius is prominently featured in the letter (1 Cor. 1:14) and might be identical with Paul's Corinthian host mentioned in Romans: "Gaius, who is host to me and to the whole church, greets you" (Rom. 16:23).

This Gaius may very well be the same person to whom 3 John is addressed and who is praised by the author of the letter for hosting traveling Christian brothers (3 John 5-8). If these connections reflect historical reality, then Gaius must have had a house large enough for the congregation. He may have been an innkeeper. But even if the mentions of Gaius in 1 Corinthians, Romans, and 3 John refer to two or three different individuals, from the perspective of a reader it is plausible that only a wealthy individual with a large home is a likely candidate to sponsor and host the dinner meetings of a Christian group.

Archaeological evidence can give us an idea of how large these dining rooms were.[7] This allows us to see what Paul and the other

7. The discussion was started by the extensive study of public meals by Matthias Klinghardt, *Gemeinschaftsmahl und Mahlgemeinschaft: Soziologie und Liturgie frühchristlicher Mahlfeiern* (Tübingen: Francke, 1996). See also Dennis E. Smith, *From Symposium to Eucharist: The Banquet in the Early Christian World* (Minneapolis: Fortress Press, 2003); Hal Taussig, *In the Beginning Was the Meal: So-*

authors of the New Testament envisioned when they designed their writings to be performed before an audience.

The images and descriptions of shared meals and symposia of the time presuppose that the participants lay down to eat.[8] One would lie on a couch with the head resting on the left arm and a cushion in the back. This way the right arm was free to take the food.[9] The dining room, called the *triclinium*, derived its name from the three couches which were typically arranged in the back of the room around a square table. On each couch there would normally be room for three or four people to lie next to each other. If the dining party was larger, several groups of three couches could be arranged in a larger dining room. It has been pointed out that a party of the host and twelve companions — i.e., the presider and twelve members of a symposium — was remarkably common and that the size of a *triclinium* typically accommodated from seven to fifteen people.[10] If the size of the group exceeded the size of the dining room, the group was divided, and one of the groups congregated in another home or another location. The greeting list in Romans 16 mentions more than thirty people, and five times a Christian household is mentioned (Rom. 16:5, 10-11, 14-15).

Sources further indicate that it was the privilege of men to lie on the couches during the meals. For women and children it was appropriate to sit either on the couch of their husbands and fathers or on low chairs *(subsellium)* placed before the host.

Lying down to eat, which in earlier times was the privilege of the nobility, was still a social marker in New Testament times. This fact is supported by an anecdote from the Roman historian Suetonius.

---

cial Experimentation and Early Christian Identity (Minneapolis: Fortress Press, 2009).

8. Klinghardt, *Gemeinschaftsmahl und Mahlgemeinschaft*, p. 75.

9. Klinghardt, *Gemeinschaftsmahl und Mahlgemeinschaft*, p. 78.

10. Klinghardt, *Gemeinschaftsmahl und Mahlgemeinschaft*, p. 77-78. Floor plans of *triclinia* can be found in this volume on pp. 591-98.

According to him, the freed slave and comedy writer Terence (Publius Terentius Afer) was at a particular event and was able to "work his way up" in the seating arrangements:[11]

> Having been introduced while Caecilius was at supper, and being meanly dressed, he [Terence] is reported to have read the beginning of the play seated on a low stool near the great man's couch. But after reciting a few verses, he was invited to take his place at table, and, having supped with his host, went through the rest to his great delight.[12]

"Being meanly dressed" seems to be the social marker requiring the freed slave Terence to sit on the small stool at first. The letter of James also refers to individuals' dress and how it might reflect the status of church members and consequently affect their place at the dining table:

> For if a person with gold rings and in fine clothes comes into your assembly, and if a poor person in dirty clothes also comes in, and if you take notice of the one wearing the fine clothes and say, "Have a seat here, please," while to the one who is poor you say, "Stand there," or, "Sit at my feet," have you not made distinctions among yourselves, and become judges with evil thoughts?
>
> James 2:2-4

Here the social conventions of the time, which involved judgment, are criticized by James.

---

11. Klinghardt, *Gemeinschaftsmahl und Mahlgemeinschaft*, p. 76.

12. Suetonius, *The Life of Terence*, trans. Alexander Thomson and Thomas Forester (London: G. Bell & Sons, 1881).

Summary

The earliest manuscripts of the Christian Bible, the archaeological evidence of the *triclinia,* and the literary evidence in the New Testament all suggest that a typical performance of a letter of Paul and, later, of other Christian literature would be heard by a group consisting of between seven and fifteen people. They would meet for a full meal in the evening, and after the meal, sacred texts would be performed as part of the worship service. Those who performed public readings of the unstructured text of the manuscripts needed to prepare in order to perform effectively, and they would typically memorize the script.

HOW PERFORMANCE CRITICISM INFORMS
THE INTERPRETATION OF THE TEXT

A Story*

Once upon a time, seven blind men lost their way in the woods. After wandering for a while, they arrived at a clearing and heard a voice say, "I am a green Helifant." The seven blind men were terrified. They had not heard of a green Helifant before.

But after a while their curiosity grew stronger than their fear, and the first blind man approached the strange creature. He touched its toes and said, "A green Helifant is very small." The second man climbed on the creature's back and shouted, "A green Helifant is very tall." The third one touched one tusk and said, "It is like a spear. It will kill us!" The fourth one touched the tail. "It is like a snake. It will bite us!" The fifth one smelled its breath and said, "It stinks like a garbage can." The sixth blind man was a very thoughtful man. He touched the toes, climbed on the back, inspected the tusk and the tail, and smelled the creature's breath, but because he was very thoughtful and did not want to jump to any conclusions, he did not say anything to anyone.

*A slightly different version of this essay was published in *The Interface of Orality and Writing: Speaking, Seeing, Writing in the Shaping of New Genres,* ed. Annette Weissenrieder and Robert B. Coote (Tübingen: Mohr Siebeck, 2010), pp. 194-201.

But the seventh blind man was like most exegetes. He was a coward. He said, "I will not go near the thing. I will analyze what it said. And it said that it is green. The *rana clamitans melanota*, the Green Frog, is green. This creature is like a frog."

"Ha, ha, ha," the green Helifant shouted. "All of you are right." And, laughing, it disappeared into the forest.

The seven blind men finally found the way back to their village. But when they talked to their neighbors, nobody would believe them. None of them had ever heard of a green Helifant. "What would that be?" they said. "A creature that is tall and small at the same time, that is like a spear, like a snake, that stinks like garbage and looks like a frog? Never have we seen anything like that. Ha, ha, ha!" The neighbors laughed and went back to their homes.

But the seven blind men knew that what they had experienced was true. They quarreled with each other by day and by night, and if they have not died, they are listening to this story.

Three Insights

What does an elusive green Helifant have to do with the scholarly exploration of texts from antiquity? Three things: Scholars are blind, scholars learn through comparison, and scholars create consensus by communicating with each other.

Scholars are blind. We cannot experience past events directly; we have to do so indirectly. Even when we examine evidence, we cannot always see the significance of it. For example, we don't understand ancient calendars and ancient currency the way we understand our own. We are like blind men and women stumbling through a forest.

Scholars learn by comparing the unknown with the known. Because we cannot find answers to our questions by looking directly at our object of interest, we compare the new evidence with evidence that we have already placed in a context. We understand by relating the unknown to what we know. The better we paint the overall picture, the easier it is for us to place a new piece of evidence.

Scholars create consensus by communicating with each other. We strive for objectivity by verifying and accepting the experiences of our colleagues as if these experiences were our own. In this regard the seven blind men in our story fail. They do not acknowledge each other's observations and therefore are stuck in eternal discussions. Only the sixth blind man has a comprehensive experience. He touches the toes, climbs on the back, inspects the tusk and tail, and smells the creature's breath, but he does not communicate his experience to the others. If an experience is not shared, it is irrelevant to the scholarly discourse. This is why publishing is an essential part of scholarship and science. The German language does not differentiate between scholarship and science: both are called *Wissenschaft.* The word references a methodological approach to observations and theory: *ein Vorgang, der Wissen schaft.*

Scholarship constructs theories from verified text observations by controlling the process through documented *exegetical methods.* Exegetical methods describe paths through the jungle of evidence, promising that if you follow the proposed methodological guidelines, the seemingly random appearances will find structure and a consistent image will emerge.

The Greek word θεωρια *(theoria)* is put together from θεα *(thea)* and οραω *(horaō).* Θεα *(thea)* can carry three meanings: the act of watching, the spectacle that is being watched, and the point from where something is watched. The basic meaning of οραω *(horaō)* is to see. In Greek literature, the word θεωρια *(theoria)* describes the experience of a spectator at a sports game or at the theatre, or in more general terms, the activity of observing and contemplating from a distance.

The connection between θέα (the view) and θεά (the Goddess) is intriguing. The words are spelled the same way but pronounced slightly differently. One of the characteristics generally attributed to the Divine is omnipresence, the ability to be everywhere at once. When scholars develop a theory, they strive to put seemingly disparate observations in a context that transcends time and place. If a theory works, it should be applicable to past and future events.

The word μεθοδος (methodos) is put together from οδος (hodos), "the path," and the preposition μετα (meta), suggesting a way around something, or a way to follow in pursuit of knowledge. In narratives the word often translates as "trick" or "ruse."

In this sense an exegetical method is a way around. It's a trick, a ruse to look at a text from a distance and study it in context in order to extract an interpretation that was not apparent at first glance.

Let me give an example. The last sentence of Luke's Gospel reads, "And they worshiped him, and returned to Jerusalem with great joy; and they were continually in the temple blessing God" (Luke 24:52-53).[1]

In some handwritten copies the Greek word for "they were blessing" is ευλογουντες (eulogountes). But another manuscript tradition uses αινουντες (ainountes). There is no significant difference in meaning between these two words. Most surviving manuscripts, however, present both readings connected with "and" αινουντες και ευλογουντες (ainountes kai eulogountes), which the translators of the King James Version rendered as "they were praising and blessing God."

On first sight these text observations may not make sense. The first edition of Luke certainly had only one of these three documented variants, didn't it? Why say the same thing twice? Why exchange a perfectly good word for another good word? And why combine two synonyms?

---

1. English quotations from the Bible are taken from the NRSV: *The Holy Bible: Containing the Old and New Testaments with the Apocryphal/Deuterocanonical Books: New Revised Standard Version* (New York: Oxford University Press, 1989).

The Gospel according to Luke is not the only writing, the New Testament is not the only collection of writings, and the Christian Bible is not the only book transmitted by hand for hundreds of years. There is a wealth of evidence available outside of the Bible. By stepping back and looking at the evidence in the larger context of book production in antiquity, a theory can be developed about why these changes were made and who typically made them. After such a contextual theory is established, it can be applied to specific passages like Luke 25:53.

Studying cases where both the master manuscript and copies of this master manuscript are extant, scholars recognized a pattern. It seems that scribes who encountered two different readings in two different copies of the same text tended to combine both by adding a conjunction.[2] This theory satisfies the observations made in Luke 24:53; only the conjunction και *(kai)*, "and," is added between the two synonyms. The technical term for such readings is *conflation,* the flowing together of two or more traditions. The guiding principle suggested by this theory is that interpreters of conflate readings should assume that conflation is younger and each one of the shorter readings is older than their combination.

A theory makes assumptions based on probability. It interprets the individual event within the context of the probable, not the possible. Probability is calculated by dividing the number of actual events with the number of possible events. The function of an exegetical method is to make an assessment of probability by studying actual events, discerning a pattern, and placing text observations within the context of this pattern.

Performance criticism as an exegetical method encourages the interpreter to place text evidence within the context of what we know about actual performances of text in antiquity.

2. Brooke Foss Westcott and Fenton John Anthony Hort, *The New Testament in the Original Greek: Introduction, Appendix* (London: Macmillan, 1896), pp. 49-52.

Performance Criticism and Form Criticism

The reading experience in antiquity differs considerably from a modern reading experience. Whereas reading is mostly a silent, solitary activity today, the manuscripts of antiquity were designed by authors, editors, and publishers to record sound; published literature was intended to serve as a script to be interpreted to an audience by a performer.[3] Form-critical approaches stress the importance of understanding the situation of communication in which a text functions, and performance criticism can provide the necessary contextual information.

"Sitz im Leben"

The Pope received a phone call from Jesus Christ. "The good news is that I have returned," Jesus said. "And the bad news?" the Pope asked. "I am calling from Salt Lake City."

Much will depend on who tells this joke and to whom. It makes a difference if a Mormon, a Catholic, a Protestant, or a Jewish person tells it. And it will make a difference who listens. The joke may mock Catholics (if a Mormon tells it to a Mormon), it may express an uneasiness with organized religion (if a Protestant tells it to a Protestant), or it may be an expression of poor taste (if a Jew tells it to a Catholic). In this context the joke simply illustrates the form-critical term *Sitz im Leben* and the importance of assessing the situation of communication. Its historical value would be mostly so-

---

3. David Trobisch, "Structural Markers in New Testament Manuscripts with Special Attention to Observations in Codex Boernerianus (G 012) and Papyrus 46 of the Letters of Paul," in *Pericope: Scripture as Written and Read in Antiquity,* vol. 5: *Layout Markers in Biblical Manuscripts and Ugaritic Tablets,* ed. Marjo C. A. Korpel and Josef M. Oesch (Assen: Koninklijke van Gorcum, 2005), pp. 177-90.

ciological, documenting attitudes of a segment of the population. To the question of whether the Pope even takes phone calls, the joke contributes little.

Performance criticism and form criticism are closely related.[4] Form criticism tries to describe how a specific text was communicated by answering questions like "Who talks to whom, where, when, and why?"

The Christian Bible is put together from texts that belong to a wide number of genres reflecting diverse communication settings. An Aramaic saying of Jesus may have changed its genre as it was translated into Greek and became part of a canonical Gospel, and the genre may have changed again as it was used by Christians in their worship services. When we read Paul's letter to Rome today, we don't read the letter that was actually carried by a trusted messenger. We read Romans, as we call it, as part of a carefully arranged and edited collection of letters. The letter has ceased to be a private communication between two parties, protected from the prying eyes of outsiders. It is now directed to the public — it has become literature.[5]

Because traditional texts tend to shift their genre as they are passed on, many German biblical scholars prefer to talk about *Form-*

4. Connections to other exegetical methods in addition to form criticism are explored by David Rhoads, "Performance Criticism: An Emerging Methodology in Second Testament Studies — Part II," *Biblical Theology Bulletin* 36 (2006): 164-84. In this essay, Rhoads, who was one of the first New Testament scholars to promote performance of biblical texts as an exegetical approach, compares performance criticism to form and genre criticisms; narrative, reader-response, and rhetorical criticisms; textual, oral, and social-science criticisms; speech act theory, linguistic criticism, and translation studies; ideological criticism, theatre, and oral interpretation studies. The author concludes that performance criticism should be seen as a discrete exegetical approach in its own right.

5. David Trobisch, "Das Neue Testament im Lichte des zweiten Jahrhunderts," *Herkunft und Zukunft der neutestamentliche Wissenschaft*, ed. Oda Wischmeyer, Neutestamentliche Entwürfe zur Theologie 6 (Tübingen, Basel: Francke, 2003), pp. 119-29.

geschichte, the history of form, rather than *Formkritik,* form criticism.[6] Keeping in mind that the function of a text may change as the historical genre of the same text shifts, performance criticism concentrates on the moment a text is published, when it stops being a private communication between specific persons and becomes a communication between an author and an undefined public. Performance criticism describes the impact of the Christian Bible as literature.

Jesus Tells a Bathroom Joke

In Matthew's Gospel, Jesus talks about hypocrites who stand at busy intersections and pray so others will see them. Jesus rebukes such practices and says, "But whenever you pray, go into your room and shut the door and pray to your Father who is in secret; and your Father who sees in secret will reward you" (Matt. 6:6). Like our homes today, houses in antiquity had at least one room that could be locked: the bathroom. Jesus was trying to be funny; his original audience was expected to laugh.

Once an interpreter accepts the form-critical assessment that this saying of Jesus may be based on a joke he made in public, the irony of the other statements in the context becomes apparent. How likely is it that a pious person would stand at a street corner and pray in order to be seen? Or that he or she would have someone "sound the trumpet" when they went to give alms "in the syna-

---

6. Martin Dibelius, *Die Formgeschichte des Evangeliums* (Tübingen: J. C. B. Mohr, 1919); Klaus Koch, *Was ist Formgeschichte?: Methoden der Bibelexegese: Mit einem Nachwort, Linguistik und Formgeschichte* (Neukirchen-Vluyn: Neukirchener Verlag, 1974); Gerd Theissen, *Urchristliche Wundergeschichten ein Beitrag zur formgeschichtlichen Erforschung der synoptischen Evangelien,* Studien zum Neuen Testament 8 (Gütersloh: Mohn, 1974); Klaus Berger, *Formgeschichte des Neuen Testaments* (Heidelberg: Quelle & Meyer, 1984).

gogues and in the streets" (Matt. 6:2)? Don't we know from our own stand-up comedians that exaggeration is part of a strategy to make us laugh at ourselves? If Jesus was joking, then the criticism of the "hypocrites" might just be a criticism from within, a call for renewal, an attempt to communicate through humor. Jesus, a pious Jew, is asking other pious Jews to return to their own ideals, to remember God's commandments and promises.

The text continues, "Your Father knows what you need before you ask him. Pray then in this way: Our Father in heaven, hallowed be your name . . ." (Matt. 6:8-9). The editor of the Sermon on the Mount, who used the saying of Jesus to introduce the Lord's Prayer, may have already missed the irony. The genre shifted from a joke to an exhortation. And in the tradition of Christian preaching, Jesus' caricature of a Pharisee has often been interpreted as disparaging Jews; it was easily turned into political propaganda. Considering the medieval pogroms and the mass murder of Jews in the twentieth century, committed by professed Christians, this misinterpretation is no laughing matter.

The Experimental Nature of Performance Criticism

In 1947 the Norwegian anthropologist Thor Heyerdahl and five other daring seafarers launched a balsa wood raft outside the port of Callào in Peru. They sailed more than 4,000 miles across the Pacific Ocean and landed on the Raroia Atoll in the Tuamotu Archipelago 101 days later.[7] The voyage demonstrated that it was possible for a primitive raft to sail the Pacific and that Polynesia was well within the range of prehistoric South American seafarers. Based on linguistic, physical, and genetic evidence, however, many anthro-

7. Thor Heyerdahl, *The Kon-Tiki Expedition: By Raft across the South Seas* (London: Allen & Unwin, 1950).

pologists remain convinced that Polynesia was settled from the Asian mainland in the West and not from South America. But some apparent American influences — like the sweet potato as part of the Polynesian diet — find a satisfactory explanation in Thor Heyerdahl's theory.

In very much the same way, performance criticism of the New Testament can demonstrate possibilities and create plausibility for new understandings that otherwise seem far-fetched. Like experimental archaeology, which recreates tools, events, and settings of the period studied, performance criticism recreates the situation of a performance of literature for which the New Testament originally had been designed. And like experimental archaeology, performance criticism can be used to test methods and theories.[8]

The Experiential Nature of Performance

In the performance of the text, the word becomes flesh. Interpreters explore possible authorial intentions, the basic structure of the argument, reactions from the audience, and subtexts of underlying humor and irony, some or all of which might have escaped their attention had they only studied the text sitting at a desk and read it quietly to themselves.

During a performance, text is simply experienced; the analysis takes place afterwards, when an emotional distance from the performance has been established. A debriefing session after the performance, preferably the following day, will typically help students reach a high level of exegetical and theological reflection.

After engaging text through performance, one often finds that

8. J. M. Coles, *Experimental Archaeology* (London: Academic Press, 1979); Daniel W. Ingersoll, John E. Yellen, and William MacDonald, *Experimental Archeology* (New York: Columbia University Press, 1977).

a specific text can be understood in more than one valid way. Like other forms of art, performance of literature will present only one of several possible interpretations, not necessarily the most authoritative one, or a scholastically viable reading. Especially in those rare cases when the setting allows for repeat performances before the same audience, and the interpreter performs the same text in several different ways, the multifaceted nature of human communication through art becomes evident. Developing a variety of possible interpretations is a crucial step of scholarly discourse; the performance of texts before an audience helps to achieve this goal.

Does Performance Criticism Oppose Historical Criticism?

Like other literary critical assessments, performance criticism may be perceived as opposing the historical-critical approach prevalent in biblical studies since the Enlightenment. This is not accurate. Whereas more traditional methods like source criticism and tradition criticism concentrate on the early stages of texts — i.e., the written sources and oral traditions that were used to weave a text together — performance criticism as a historical approach concentrates on the moment the finished literary product is presented to the public for the first time. Obviously, the authorial intention at the time of publication is limited to the implied author's intention as promoted by the publisher, and does not necessarily represent the original message of the historical author.

For example, in the New Testament, Acts is presented as the account of Luke (Acts 1:1-2 references the Third Gospel), the account of Paul's travel companion (see the "we" passages in Acts 28:11ff.), and the account of the physician (Col. 4:14), who finishes his narrative while Paul is still alive (Acts 28:30-31). Each of these statements is contested on historical grounds. But at the same time, if the implied author and the implied literary setting are dismissed, the text will not function as it was designed to function when published.[9]

Furthermore, historical-critical approaches tend to concentrate their efforts on genuine material only. They are interested in the historical author and audience. One of the strengths of any literary approach, including performance criticism, is to give spurious material the voice it deserves. Spurious writings are an attempt, sometimes a desperate attempt, to contextualize a cherished tradition, to reinterpret it, to make it meaningful for an audience at a time and place quite different from the original setting of the writing.

Summary

Performance criticism takes the character of New Testament texts as Hellenistic literature seriously. As a historical method, it recreates the situation for which these texts were designed and encourages the interpreting performer to experiment and explore multiple possibilities of authorial intention, structure, argument, and audience reactions through the act of performing the text before an audience. As a literary approach it encourages the student to appreciate the beauty of the New Testament as literature.

9. David Trobisch, "Die narrative Welt der Apostelgeschichte," *ZNT* 18 (2006): 9-14; David Trobisch, "The Book of Acts as a Narrative Commentary on the Letters of the New Testament: A Programmatic Essay," in *Rethinking the Unity and Reception of Luke and Acts,* ed. Andrew F. Gregory and C. Kavin Rowe (Columbia: University of South Carolina Press, 2010), pp. 119-27.

PERFORMANCE TODAY:
FROM PREPARATION TO REVIEW

A Story

Years ago I (David) visited a friend in Heidelberg, Germany, who happened to have a visitor, a professor from Israel. When the Israeli colleague heard that I was interested in literary approaches to biblical literature, he told me the following story.

The literature department at his university conducted an experiment. They divided the incoming class into three groups. The first group attended a lecture by a young scholar who had written his dissertation on a contemporary poet. He talked about the life of the writer, his publications, and the critical reception his works received. The second group was not told anything about the author, but listened as a renowned performer presented the poems. The third group was invited to memorize, rehearse, and perform selected poems before an audience. The university assessed the outcomes, and it turned out that the members of the third group had achieved a much deeper critical appreciation of the poet's work than their colleagues had.

I never met this professor again, and I don't know where and when or even if this experiment really happened, but after teaching many workshops, I know that the story is true.

THE FOLLOWING section contains practical advice for those who plan a performance of a biblical text and who want to walk a group through the process from the moment they engage with the text to the point when they perform it before an audience.

Engaging the Script

As organizers of the performance, always keep in mind that you only facilitate what the group has to offer. It is important that the directors, as we will call the persons in charge, are not "front and center." The performance of a biblical text shouldn't be about them or about the audience, but about engaging with the text. From our experience, those who benefit the most from this exercise are those who perform the text.

Often performers find that they cannot prepare the presentation of a biblical text as a group, so they need to work individually. Following the steps outlined here will be helpful. (The steps for individual performances are the same.)

Advertise the Performance

From the outset, create awareness that the sessions are geared to facilitate a performance before an audience. Make sure that the participants know the date and location of the venue, and that they are available to perform.

Here's an example. Richard and I taught a one-week, three-credit summer course in Bangor, Maine. Even before we met with the class, we had sent around announcements to local churches that they had printed in their respective Sunday bulletins, inviting parishioners to the former Unitarian Church to a re-enactment of "Paul's Letter to the Philippians" on Friday evening. At our first meeting on Monday morning, we recruited three students to form the "welcome committee." The committee took responsibility for creating and distributing posters, making phone calls, and sending e-mails to reach people who might be interested in our performance. The evening of the performance, the welcome committee greeted visitors at the door and ushered them in. Having invited an audience even before we had finalized the script created a sense of urgency and helped the group to focus on the final outcome of our week together: the performance on Friday evening.

Establish the Script

We usually present the group with the script at the first meeting. It isn't necessary to include the whole group in the process of establishing the script. Any text from the Bible is worth performing. Participants may propose changes, additions, or cuts to the script and discuss such proposals with the group. Often these changes do not require a new hard copy. And, should the group decide to go with a different script, the decision is greatly facilitated when everyone holds the proposed text in hand.

Decisions about the script have to be made boldly. The amount of text that can be performed depends mostly on the participants' abilities and commitment of time. We found that expecting each individual involved to do two or three sentences from memory works well.

As far as the form of the script is concerned, it is a good idea to keep it simple. We suggest providing computer-generated printouts with minimal paragraphing and no chapter and verse numbers, headings, or stage instructions, mimicking the script an ancient reader of the New Testament would have had in his or her hands when, for example, presenting a text to a congregation.

Below we give a few examples of the different kinds of scripts we prepared for different groups.

Performing Galatians: A Chance for Summer Congregants to Learn Performance

A congregation in Maine had a tradition of offering learning opportunities to their summer guests. They invited me (David) for a three-day workshop. A group of four couples committed to meeting every afternoon for three hours and preparing a performance for the evening of the last day. A shared breakfast the morning after the presentation would conclude our time together. The pastor suggested we engage with Paul's letter to the Galatians because this seemed to be such a difficult text to understand, and guidance from a New Testament professor would be greatly appreciated.

I used a contemporary translation (CEV) to encourage a new hearing of a familiar text. Additionally, I changed the translation slightly by replacing the term "Jew" with "Jews living in Judea" and the term "Gentiles" with "Jews living outside of Judea" to drive home the point that this letter documents an inner Jewish controversy. This was a change that I felt was necessary on exegetical grounds, a change that the group and I discussed thoroughly during our rehearsal time. For this script, I eliminated verse and chapter numbers and structured the text by paragraphs. Because it was clear that the entire letter couldn't be performed with such limited preparation time, I chose the conflict between Paul and Jerusalem as the red thread, concentrating on the first two chapters supported by a small selection of passages from chapters three through six.

Performing Philippians: Academic Course (3 credits)

This class was performing Philippians. To make the script, David and I printed the relatively brief text on two pages and glued them together to form a scroll. We gave a copy to all the participants. Although they could mark up their personal exemplar, we told them that the scroll to be used during the performance would have no notes on it; it would serve as a prop only. They would present the text from memory.

Performing the Gospel of Mark: Academic Course (4 credits)

For a public performance of the Gospel of Mark, I (Richard) divided the text so that each member of the class of sixteen would have three or four sections of the text (of six to eight lines each). After studying and rehearsing the text, we performed it as an ensemble on two occasions, once in the multi-purpose room of the seminary and once in the seminary library. Using the New Revised Standard Version, we performed the entire Gospel of Mark.

Performance of Text and Sermon: Academic Course (3 credits)

This course that I (Richard) taught was offered as a two-week intensive class. During the first week, students worked on their assigned texts, performing the Gospel at the end of the week. During the second week, students chose one of the performed texts and developed a sermon as a response to that text. So, the first week they followed and performed the script of Mark, and the second week they wrote and performed a script of their own.

Internalize the Script

The best way to make a text meaningful to an audience is to make it meaningful to the performers. In antiquity, performances from manuscripts that contained *scriptio continua* and *nomina sacra* required the readers to familiarize themselves with the script beforehand.

There are many different ways to approach a new script, and with experience, performers will find what works best for them. A very common approach is to write out the text by hand or to type it into a computer. Many report that a motor activity like walking helps their memorization. Often participants say that reading the script out loud repeatedly — exploring the text through their ears — helps them to structure the flow of sound by adding pauses; it triggers emotional responses and encourages performers to play with different intonations. Still others read silently and highlight specific words and passages, sometimes using highlighting markers. As performers physically experience words through these activities, they resolve structural questions as they arise.

But it's important to remember that memorization isn't the goal; it's only the first step. Performing is about delivering a message.

An Exercise in Memory and Performance

After presenting the group with a script, divide the group into smaller groups of three or four participants each. If the text to be performed is long, break it up into sections of three to five verses, with one section assigned to each group. If the text to be performed is short, all groups can work with the same passage.

The first step is to instruct the small groups to first read the paragraph silently and then read it aloud to each other until everyone has read it out loud at least three times. Encourage the readers to experiment with intonation and pauses.

The second step is to put the script away and let everyone tell the story in her or his own words, but without embellishment. Encourage the participants to be faithful to the story without necessarily being literal. Again, everyone does this three times.

The next step is to have everyone read the text again, pick a significant sentence, and memorize it. For this part of the exercise, participants may want to stand up, walk around, and say the sentence out loud to themselves. When the small groups come together, each participant tells the story in his/her own words, but when he or she reaches the memorized sentence, he or she says that sentence literally. Everyone tells his/her story only once. This performance, which should take between fifteen and twenty minutes, concludes the exercise.

About Memorization

During our workshops, we (Richard and I) usually hand out the script and instruct participants to memorize it without elaborating how they should do this. Instead, we give them time to do it — typically overnight — and then give everyone an opportunity to talk about their experience when we meet again. Sharing different approaches deflects frustration, provides fresh ideas, and encourages experimenting. Every person is different, and there is no miraculous technique that will work for everyone.

To distinguish "memorization" from "rote recitation," we use the term "internalization" to describe the goal of the process: for everyone to speak the words of a text as if they are his/her own. There is rarely a complete correspondence between what the performer speaks and the words on a page. Yet a listener should be able to recognize the literary text in the performer's words.

Memorizing has to be done individually. It isn't a group activity. Sometimes participants can be asked to memorize a short text before the first meeting; sometimes letting them work overnight is the better option. In a classroom setting, you can assign class time to memorizing, but ask each student to find space alone to do this. Many prefer to leave the room and walk as they try to commit their text to memory.

Under no circumstances should this step be skipped. The temptation to relieve participants of making an effort to memorize the text is usually enormous. But memorization is at the heart of internalizing a text, of making it one's own.

Strategies for Memorization

In the vast majority of participants' experiences, the breaking of a text into at least three but no more than seven units is the single most important aid to memorization. Once participants understand the overall flow of a text, they overcome a big hurdle. Others report that they mark the first three words of every sentence and only memorize those words. They say that once they start a sentence correctly, the rest of it falls into place for them. Others observe that walking the dog, taking a shower, or any other kind of repetitive physical activity helps them memorize the text. It seems that the distraction creates memory at a deeper level of consciousness.

Below are some other exercises that we find helpful.

Working with Visuals (David) ──────────────

As a teenager, I learned to use visuals as an aid to remember sequences. I imagine myself standing in the fully furnished living room of the home where I grew up. The first visual image I put in the first corner to the left, the next image I put on the wall to the left, the third one I place in the next corner, and so on. The ninth visual image sits on the floor in the middle of the room, and the last image, number ten, I attach to the ceiling. If I have more than ten images, I enter the next room and repeat the process. Finally, if necessary, I walk around the house and place items outside each corner and wall. Because our home had nine rooms, I am able to place one hundred reminders in a sequence. This technique guarantees that I won't leave out any essential content. And when I perform a text in another language, I use the same visuals.

Here's an example: "*Early in the morning* [as a symbol for the rising sun, I place the reproduction of Van Gogh's *Sunflowers*, which my mother loved so much, in the first corner], *Jesus came again to the temple* [on the piano, which stood along the left wall of our living room, I place a little model of the Jerusalem temple], *and he sat down* [in my imagination I move one of our living room chairs into the next corner]." And I continue the process until every sequence in my passage has a visual image.

Using Parts to Internalize John 8:2-11 (David)

Early in the morning he came again to the temple. All the people came to him, and he sat down and began to teach them. The scribes and the Pharisees brought a woman who had been caught in adultery; and making her stand before all of them, they said to him, "Teacher, this woman was caught in the very act of committing adultery. Now in the law Moses commanded us to stone such women. Now what do you say?" They said this to test him, so that they might have some charge to bring against him. Jesus bent down and wrote with his finger on the ground. When they kept on questioning him, he straightened up and said to them, "Let anyone among you who is without sin be the first to throw a stone at her." And once again he bent down and wrote on the ground. When they heard it, they went away, one by one, beginning with the elders; and Jesus was left alone with the woman standing before him. Jesus straightened up and said to her, "Woman, where are they? Has no one condemned you?" She said, "No one, sir." And Jesus said, "Neither do I condemn you. Go your way, and from now on do not sin again."

1. First, I take the story of Jesus and the adulteress and break it up into three parts. (I would suggest these three: Jesus arrives; the Pharisees and scribes question him; Jesus responds.)

2. Next, I take the first part, write down the first three words of every sentence, and memorize them by counting them off with my fingers or by visualizing the action as I rehearse. ("Early in the morning . . . All the people . . . The scribes and . . . 'Teacher, this woman . . . Now in the . . . Now what do . . .' They said this . . .")

3. Finally, I try to tell the first part of the story by using the sentence beginnings and slowly filling in the wording of the script as I repeat the effort.

4. When I feel confident about my grasp of part one, I take a short break and then move on to parts two and three, repeating the steps.

Using Episodes (Richard) ————————————————————

Because I'm not a visual learner, I follow some guidelines proposed by the International Network of Biblical Storytellers (www.nbs.org). I take the text, strip it of chapters, verses, and headings, and break it up into narrative units called "episodes" of three to four lines each. I try to work on one episode at a time, moving from one to the next until I'm able to stitch the episodes together into a coherent flow. In the case of an Epistle, I identify "thought units" of two or three lines each and note where they shift. I find that getting up and moving around gets the text into my body and helps me find the energy that I experience in front of an audience.

About Gestures

The audience not only listens to the voices of the performers, but also observes their movements. Memorizing is often difficult and unpleasant. To think of and rehearse at least one supporting gesture often alleviates the discomfort. Participants should develop the gesture themselves and rehearse it until it feels natural to them. Gestures should suggest an action (such as looking over the shoulders of people in front of them in a crowd) or an attitude (such as crossed arms indicating disdain) in the text. Encourage all performers to think of and rehearse at least one gesture as they internalize the script. Encourage them to watch themselves in a mirror as they rehearse.

Example: Jesus and the Adulterous Woman ————————————

Early in the morning. . . . As a performer you could be stretching, moving your head slowly from side to side, yawning.

Jesus came again to the temple. . . . You could walk into the audience, acknowledging the listeners by nodding your head or reaching out with both arms and shaking hands. Gestures like this acknowledge the audience and assign the listeners a role during the performance. Do you want them to be active bystanders, witnessing the exchange? Or should they identify with Jesus as you tell the story? Or should they identify with the scribes and Pharisees? Your gestures will effectively assign them a role.

As you rehearse the story, try different movements and gestures as you recite different lines: "he sat down and began to teach them"; "he bent down and wrote on the ground"; "Jesus straightened up and said to her. . . ." Your gestures will help your audience understand your interpretation of the story and encourage them to find their own.

About Intonation and Pause

One of the signs that a performer has internalized a text is that he or she has decided about correct intonation and where to create pauses. Questions end in a higher pitch than pure statements. And even questions vary in intonation and intensity. You could be calmly asking a friend you haven't seen for a while, "What did you do?" Or you could be yelling "What did you do?!" as your cat proudly drops the bloody remains of a mouse on the living room carpet. In the pause after the question, you invite a range of imaginary reactions depending on how you've asked the question.

Exercise

Performers tend to make Jesus' voice tender and soft, full of patience and understanding. But try to say his words differently — as a rebuke, as an angry retort. If the adulterous woman was caught "in the very act," then why wasn't the man brought as well? Imagine for a moment that this man is the one who asks the questions. How would you feel? Consider how you would say this crucial sentence: "Let anyone among you who is without sin be the first to throw a stone at her." Try shouting the sentence. Try whispering it.

The Components of a Story

Once the script is memorized, it's a good idea to step back and analyze the story. Every story typically contains a mix of four components: perspective, setting, characters, and conflict.

Perspective

As you explore a biblical story, try to understand the perspective from which the story is told. Let's use Matthew 1:18-21 as an example:

> When his mother Mary had been engaged to Joseph, but before they lived together, she was found to be with child from the Holy Spirit. Her husband Joseph, being a righteous man and unwilling to expose her to public disgrace, planned to dismiss her quietly. But just when he had resolved to do this, an angel of the Lord appeared to him in a dream and said, "Joseph, son of David, do not be afraid to take Mary as your wife, for the child conceived in her is from the Holy Spirit. She will bear a son, and you are to name him Jesus, for he will save his people from their sins."

The narrative voice tells the story from Joseph's perspective. Information is shared with the audience that only Joseph could have known: his sexual abstinence from his fiancée and the particulars of the dream he had. So, as you re-tell the story, you take Joseph's point of view; as you perform, you "become" Joseph for a moment.

Settings

Break the passage down in settings, noting when place and time change. If you filmed the story, how often would you have to set up the camera in different places, at different times? In the above example there are at least two settings. The first setting is when it was "found" that Mary was pregnant and Joseph made his decision "to dismiss her quietly." When, where, and how this happened is not elaborated. The second setting is when Joseph sleeps and has a dream, clearly a different time and place than the first setting.

Characters

Make sure that you're aware of the characters. How many persons interact with each other? Is the narrator one of the characters in the story? For this story, it's important that the audience is familiar with the characters of Mary, Joseph, and Jesus in order to understand the narrative. And, one might argue, they should also be prepared to accept the "Lord" as a character in the story; he speaks through another character, a messenger, "an angel of the Lord."

As the story continues, you'll notice the narrator. He's introduced to readers as Matthew through the title of this book; later, he'll be identified as a tax collector (Matt. 9:9) and one of the twelve disciples of Jesus (Matt. 10:3). In two subsequent verses he addresses the audience of this story directly:

All this took place to fulfill what had been spoken by the Lord through the prophet: "Look, the virgin shall conceive and bear a son, and they shall name him Emmanuel," which means "God is with us." (Matt. 1:22-23)

By interpreting the action and creating a reference to a prophetic statement, the narrator becomes a character of the story as well. And because he steps out of the story-world and talks directly to readers, his audience also become characters. They are passive bystanders, witnessing the unfolding events and trying to connect them to their own lives in a meaningful way.

Conflict

Every story will have a conflict that moves the plot along. In its purest form, a conflict has two parties; each of these parties is "right" when the events are seen through their eyes and experienced from their point of view. At first sight, however, it seems impossible to resolve the disagreement between the parties.

Often the conflict is based on individual decisions that create a tension with the community. For example, a man kills another man in self-defense. (This action is justifiable by the standards of the community.) Then he meets the man's widow, falls in love with her, and marries her. (This action is honorable, based on mutual love and commitment.) Years later, the husband discovers that the man he killed was his father. (Killing one's father is one of the most terrible crimes imaginable.) The woman he married is therefore his own mother. (Sleeping with a parent is a sexual aberration that cannot be tolerated by the community.) Although, from the perspective of the hero, the things he did were justifiable and honorable (given the circumstances as he knew them), the outcome is unacceptable by the hero's own moral standards and the standards of the community in which he lives. This is the conflict on which the tragedy of King Oedipus is based.

What is the conflict in the story of Joseph? Why does he consider dismissing his fiancée quietly? Why does the dream resolve the situation for him? As storyteller, you will have to make a choice. It is important that you decide on one of the possible conflicts in order to tell the story effectively. As a general rule, the stronger the conflict, the better the story.

Three Approaches to Performing the Script

A performance doesn't have to follow the script literally to be recognized as a faithful rendering of the biblical witness. There are three basic possibilities:

1. Following the text closely and interpreting it through gestures and movement.
2. Staying within the narrative world of the story, but telling the story in one's own words, exploring the background of the events, switching perspectives, adding detail, and embellishing.
3. Placing the conflict of the narrative in a contemporary setting.

Speaking the Text

Some performance settings require a literal rendering of the biblical text. A congregation may be heavily invested in a specific translation for denominational reasons and may not tolerate the lectionary reading from any other source. Conservative groups may insist on the King James Version; the New Revised Standard Version may be the only accepted standard translation in congregations with sensitivity to gender language; and still other congregations may use a very specific contemporary translation for their youth work. If the exact text is a given, performers will offer explanation and commentary through gestures and movement.

Several times I (David) have done the lectionary reading in congregations where the parishioners were used to reading along in the church bulletin. If the setting allowed it, I stepped away from the lectern and walked down to the pews. Everyone could see that I wasn't reading from a book. I tried to establish eye contact and then recited the lectionary text. Again and again I saw people look at me, then look at the bulletin, and then at me again, baffled that I was saying exactly what they had on their page. "I don't know how you can memorize so much text" is one of the most common compliments I've received. And I may only have performed three simple sentences!

Parishioners that I've interacted with have often been surprised by how well our translations read. And when their eyes almost invariably moved away from the bulletin and rested on me, following my movements, studying my gestures, I took it as a sign that I had earned their trust. Being trusted is a prerequisite for effective story-telling.

"When will you preach again?" a woman asked me after a service. I had not preached; I had only done the Gospel reading. But for her it was as important as the sermon.

Example: John 8:2-11: "Making her stand before all of them" ───────

In the story of Jesus and the adulterous woman, the scribes and Pharisees brought her to him and "[made] her stand before all of them" (NRSV). In this particular instance, the performer of the text was walking along the pews. At this point, he gestured to a female parishioner to stand up and walk with him to the altar. Then, without saying a word, he turned her around and "made her stand before all of them."

At the point in the story when the elders, scribes, and Pharisees left the scene and Jesus asked, "Woman, where are they? Has no one condemned you?" the performer whispered to the woman, "Say, 'No one, sir.'" Then he began with "She said," and the parishioner continued, "No one, sir." In response, the performer addressed the woman: "And Jesus said, 'Neither do I condemn you.'"

At this point the performer turned to the audience and placed himself between the woman and the congregation, as if to protect "her" from "them." He looked at the people in the pews, and, meeting the eyes of individuals, he raised both arms and blessed them, sending them home with the words "Go your way, and from now on do not sin again."

Without changing the translation, the performer conveyed the message of the story he decided to deliver that morning to that audience: The story wasn't about the woman who had done wrong; it was about those who condemned her. Although the listeners would have been aware that in the narrative Jesus spoke the last sentence to the adulterous woman, the performer opened them up to another way of reading the story, one that may have made them uncomfortable as they sat in the pews watching one of their own "made to stand before all of them."

Example: Mark 16: A Ragged Ending

One of my (Richard's) students was exploring different ways to tell the end of the Gospel of Mark. After Mary Magdalene and two other women discover that Jesus' tomb is empty, they encounter an anonymous young man who tells them to inform the disciples. The Gospel closes with this sentence: "And they said nothing to anyone, for they were afraid" (ἐφοβοῦντο γάρ; Mark 16:8). The Gospel ends with a conjunction, the Greek word γάρ, breaking literary conventions that would ask for a continuation of the story. And really — could one think of a worse ending to a Gospel than "They didn't tell anyone"?

How does someone perform a text that ends as this one does?

How does one perform the "ragged" ending of the Gospel of Mark? The student decided to slightly change the sequence of words as she spoke the final sentence: "They were afraid, for . . ." Then she gave a slight shrug of her shoulders. The gesture reflected the open-ended effect of the text and offered the insight that the "ending" of Mark is not a word but a performer's gesture.

Saying It with Our Own Words

There are many ways to get the message of the biblical text across other than a literal rendering of a printed translation, and every performer will express his or her own voice in different ways. This can be a challenge. It's no coincidence that our best-trained performers, our actors in theatre and film, are expected to follow a script. It's difficult for a performer to make someone else's words sound as if he or she had written them, and the effort benefits from professional training. But we need to remember that performers in an early Christian setting weren't professional actors.

Actually, there was and still is a sense that acting is inappropriate in church. The Greek word for "actor" is *hypokritēs,* from which the English word "hypocrite" derives, describing "one who pretends to be what he is not." The negative connotation is obvious. Paul uses the term when he embarrasses Peter before the congregation in Antioch for not living up to the standards of Christ and preaching one thing but doing something else (Gal. 2:13). Perhaps the most important message we can take away from this is that performing a biblical text amounts to nothing if the performance is pretentious.

Translating from English into English

In workshops Richard and I often encounter people who are frustrated because they feel that a sentence or a phrase of the traditional translation doesn't flow well. They want to move the adverb to a different place, break up one long sentence into several shorter ones, or simply replace an awkward term with a more familiar one. Others want to introduce colloquial language in dialogues or use expressions that only work regionally and so wouldn't be appropriate for a widely distributed printed version of the text.

Adapting a published translation to the language a performer is comfortable with and the language his or her audience understands is easily justified. The New Testament and the Christian Old Testament were first published in Greek. But readers know that the Jewish Scriptures were originally written in Hebrew, and that Jesus spoke Aramaic when he died on the cross (Matt. 27:46; Mark 15:34). The Greek Christian Bible therefore conveyed to its readers that it was a translation — and one can always improve on the flow of a translation. That holds true today; Richard and I call it "translating from English into English."

Example: Two Ways of Performing John 8:2-11

A performer trying to tell the story with his or her own words could rephrase the beginning of the story of Jesus and the adulterous woman the following way:

> Early one morning Jesus came to the temple. Everyone gathered around him, so he sat down and began to teach them. The scribes and the Pharisees brought a woman who had had an affair. They forced her to stand before the crowd. Then they said to Jesus, "This woman was caught having sex with a man she isn't married to . . ."

Compare this version to the translation offered in the NRSV:

> Early in the morning he came again to the temple. All the people came to him and he sat down and began to teach them. The

84

scribes and the Pharisees brought a woman who had been caught in adultery; and making her stand before all of them, they said to him, "Teacher, this woman was caught in the very act of committing adultery . . ."

Both versions are adequate representations of the underlying Greek text, which in itself captures a dialogue that would have taken place in Aramaic. In addition, this story isn't part of the oldest existing New Testament manuscripts, but was added by scribes later.[1] So, if this scene went through different hands, which translated it from Aramaic into Greek, and added it to manuscripts as they revised the New Testament, why shouldn't a performer have license to change the wording of a particular English translation?

But even if the setting demands that a traditional translation be followed, it is always a good exercise to speak the text in your own words as you familiarize yourself with the flow of the story or the flow of the argument in a biblical text.

Exploring the Background of the Events

When Bible stories are told to children, storytellers often stay in the world of the narrative but add detail, embellish, or imagine events which the text doesn't cover but which seem plausible to both performer and audience. I (David) vividly remember how my Sunday school teacher told the story of the tax collector Zacchaeus (Luke 19:1-9).

---

1. Following the tradition of Byzantine manuscripts, most translations have the story after John 7:52. Other manuscripts have it after John 7:36, others after John 21:25, and others after Luke 21:38 or Luke 24:53. The oldest manuscripts lack the story completely. See the apparatus of *Novum Testamentum Graece*, 26th edition, 1981. The story is first referenced by Papias (Eusebius, *historia ecclesiae* 3.39.17), who wrote during the first half of the second century CE.

You see, I am a little man. When there are a lot of people around, I can't see anything. So I climbed up a tree and had a good look. And when Jesus walked by, he called to me and said, "Zach, come down from that tree! I have something to tell you!"

Now, my Sunday school teacher was a tall woman, not a little man like Zacchaeus. But the way she told the story, "Zach" became our size, the size of children, and we were immediately drawn into the narrative world, because we were small, we often felt left out in large crowds, and we all loved to climb trees.

Academic preachers often introduce historical insights as they paint the canvas on which to place the story; they may talk about ancient practices, historical events, and geographical, botanical, or archaeological facts. Or, if so inclined, they may walk the audience through the history of the text's dogmatic interpretation. By doing this, they become storytellers as well, providing a framework that will favor specific interpretations over other ways of understanding the text. Often preachers will choose to convey this information through lecture-style discourse. We encourage preachers to experiment and — after a lectionary text has been read as part of the liturgy — tell the story in their own words during the sermon and incorporate whatever background information they found useful into the narrative framework.

Switching Perspectives

The Sunday school teacher told the story of Zacchaeus from the point of view of a character in the narrative. She added details that only "Zach the tax collector" could know. This allowed her to explore, for example, the emotional response of this character to the events. She also could have chosen to tell the story from Jesus' perspective.

Telling the story by switching perspectives — choosing the point of view of different characters — often de-familiarizes a familiar story and opens the ears of both performer and audience as they explore and experience a familiar text anew. This is almost always a useful exercise yielding surprising insights. What if, for example, in the story of Jesus and the adulterous woman, the woman's lover is the one who asked the question? What if this was a setup, as the text indicates: "They said this to test him" (John 8:6)?

The woman could tell the story of her encounter with Jesus from her own perspective:

> One morning my lover, a scribe by profession, dragged me out of bed and made me stand before a crowd in the temple. He pointed his finger at me and said to the teaching Rabbi, "This woman is having an affair with a man she isn't married to." The whole thing was a joke. But the Rabbi ignored him and the rest of the crowd.

Or she could tell it from the perspective of a Pharisee:

> "In our marriage counseling, we sometimes face a situation in which the wife has been unfaithful. The Bible tells us to kill such a woman. But it takes two to be unfaithful. Why not kill the man also? And anyway, the Roman government doesn't allow us to apply the death penalty without going through their courts. We can't ignore the Law of Moses, but we can't ignore the law of the land, either. What should we do? What do you say?" This was a trick question. The theologians were hoping that Jesus would oppose Roman law, which would allow them to deliver him to the authorities and get rid of him.

Exercise ————————————————————————————

Try further exploring the story of Jesus and the adulterous woman. Tell the story using the voice of a bystander, or of the woman's sister, husband, mother, or child.

Placing the Story in a Contemporary Setting

Some biblical storytellers excel when they re-tell a story by setting it in the time and place of their audience and finding a contemporary conflict that's comparable to the conflict addressed in the story. Pastors preparing sermons try to bridge the gap between the biblical text and their Sunday-morning audience. Introducing the listeners to the narrative reach of the text is an approach that works as well with people who like to engage intellectually as it does with those among us who experience spirituality on a deeply emotional level.

Example ───────────────────────────────────────

How do you shift in time and place? A simple technique is to be blunt and let the main character of the story enter the contemporary situation of the performance. Try using the story of Jesus and the adulterous woman again. The introduction, the setting of the scene, is reflected in the line "Early in the morning, Jesus came again to the temple." It could be performed this way:

> One day Jesus came again. And of all the places he could have gone, he came to Faith Church of Christ in Muscatine, Iowa. It was a Sunday morning, and the congregation had prayed their prayers, had sung their hymns, and had read the lectionary of the day. They were waiting for the sermon when the wide doors in the back flew open and Jesus walked in.

Of course, the contemporary elements could be much subtler and could be worked into the original narrative setting:

> The scribes and the Pharisees brought a Roman soldier and made him stand before all of them. They pointed to him and said, "This government has ruined us in eight long years. It has

waged war against a country that did not attack us. It has ruined our economy. It has depleted our retirement accounts, and it has killed more than four thousand of our best young people while slaughtering one hundred thousand innocent men, women, and children. But the Bible teaches us that every government is instituted by God, and that those who protest will incur judgment! What do you say?"

Here's another example:

When the local churches heard that Jesus had come and was preaching — of all places — in the Unitarian Church, they sent their pastors. The Baptist minister, the Episcopal priest, and even a Mormon preacher came. They brought two women and made them stand before all of them.

"These women," the Baptist minister said, "have been living together for twenty years. They have been faithful to each other, have been good members of our community, and when a thirteen-year-old niece gave birth to a baby boy, they took the baby and raised him as their own. They have done nothing wrong. Yet, the Bible teaches us to kill homosexuals. What do you say?"

Narrative commentaries usually work by de-familiarizing a well-known story. This is their strength. To have the adulterous woman be represented by a philandering man, a promiscuous teenager, a homosexual priest, or a mother in love with another woman's husband — any of these twists in the story will create surprise and, hopefully, open up new ways of hearing the all-too-familiar biblical tale.

The goal of a performer is to find his or her own voice. Maybe your talent is to familiarize yourself with a traditional translation so well that the sentences sound as if you had formulated them yourself. Maybe you feel most comfortable when you simply re-phrase the story in your own words. Or maybe your gift is to take a Bible text and place it in our time, addressing true conflict in your life and in the lives of your listeners. If you feel up to a big chal-lenge, try telling the same story in different versions told by differ-ent people, with one performance following the other.

Exercise ──

1. Use the text that we've been discussing: John 8:2-11. Follow the printed translation word by word. Think of gestures, move-ments, and different intonations, and rehearse them. Think of a way to include your audience in the performance.

2. Tell the biblical story in your own words, but stay in the narra-tive world of the text. Add details, elaborating on the thoughts of the Pharisees and scribes and the woman. Tell the story from different perspectives: how the woman experienced it, how her lover experienced it, how a scribe experienced it.

3. Place the story in a contemporary setting. Make sure to find a comparable conflict, something that might anger a person of faith but is not punishable under current law: abortion, homo-sexual conduct, not being truthful to your children.

Rehearsing

My (David's) mother was a gifted speaker. She used to say, "There are only three rules to public speaking: rehearse, rehearse, and rehearse!" She was right. And usually there are three stages of rehearsal.

First, an individual will have to spend time with the text on his or her own. Many say that this is the most difficult part for them when they prepare a performance. But, at the same time, having internalized a Bible text feels satisfying and is rewarding.

After individual study, it's time to rehearse in small groups. Usually this is where the group develops a life of its own, where concepts are brought forward and tested. The directors shouldn't be with each group all the time, but should grant them some privacy. Ideally, the small group will now begin to own the text and make decisions about how to contextualize the message. At this stage of the process, enormous creative energies are set free — a group may decide to speak a recurring sentence in unison or sing part of the text. At one of our workshops, a participant offered a liturgical dance as part of the performance. Other groups decided to have one person recite the text while the other group members acted out a pantomime, placing the story in a contemporary setting. Some have used symbolic props. One group used a clown's cap that they passed around, with each member putting it on for his or her performance. Another group used a simple shawl. Male speakers draped it over their heads to indicate that they had slipped into the role of a woman.

Finally, if the performing group is so large that it was divided up into smaller groups, it is necessary to bring everyone together and ensure that everyone understands how the different parts come together. Rehearsing this way motivates individuals to continue to practice their parts, and observing their colleagues' efforts inspires the small groups to try out something that they may not have thought of before.

At this stage it's important that the directors are present to facilitate group dynamics, give encouragement, and lift up the promising ideas without putting down the not-so-good ones. This is the time to encourage, not to criticize, to create a safe environment while helping the group make positive decisions about the direction they want to take in their performance. These meetings should also be used to make final decisions about where the performance should be, how to set up the stage, and exactly how long the performance will take.

Example: Paul's Letter to the Philippians

While rehearsing their performance, the group decided to recreate a situation reminiscent of the first reading of this letter in Philippi. After listening to the different exegetical theories, the group decided to think of Paul as being imprisoned in Rome. This allowed them to make a series of decisions. To begin with, the audience for that evening would be greeted by ushers when they arrived; they would be welcomed as members of the congregation in Philippi and encouraged to participate freely in the activities. In addition, the group decided not to speak from the stage, but to sit among the audience members. The small groups then decided where they wanted to sit — if they wanted to sit together or get up from different places.

After time and place were settled, the participants slipped into their chosen characters: Epaphroditus, the letter carrier; Syntyche and Euodia, who had a dispute with each other; Paul's travel companions; bishops and deacons of the congregation; a visitor from Rome; and so on. During the performance, a man from the audience spontaneously identified himself as a Roman lawyer and provided some ad hoc information on Paul's legal status. This response was unscripted and came as a surprise, but because it fit the imagined scenario of a first reading of the letter in Philippi so perfectly, the performers, staying in character, were able to ad-lib excellent responses.

The group decided to construct the conflict from Philippians 1:15-17, where Paul mentions other Christian missionaries who are happy about the fact that Paul is in prison. At the point where Paul calls his opponents "lazy workers, castrated dogs," the group decided to stage a shouting match, interrupting the reading of Paul's letter. During the rehearsal, the group took a vote on who sided with Paul and who didn't. And his opponents turned out to be loud and outspoken; how could Paul pretend to be an apostle sent by Christ when he had never met Jesus?

THE FINAL rehearsal before the performance is an opportunity to demonstrate techniques that will open up the voice, a chance to teach breathing and stretching exercises, and a time to help group members interact — shouting, whispering, stomping, lying down and helping each other get up again, leaning back-to-back against each other, singing together, and so on. It's important to create a relaxed atmosphere and help the group focus not on themselves but on the message they want to convey.

The dress rehearsal should run through the whole performance with as few unscheduled interruptions as possible. It's important to experience the flow of the performance. This is the time to make final decisions, but it's best to interrupt the performance only at points where the script suggests a break, and no more than once or twice.

There is one exception, however: the beginning and the end of the performance should be rehearsed several times until everyone is familiar with it. If participants are comfortable at the start, they will be confident, and if the end runs smoothly, the performers and the audience will quickly forget any bumps along the way.

Framing is an important help for performers and audience alike. It signals when they step into the narrative world of the text, and when they step out again. It's a good idea to include the audience in a brief liturgical exchange. Use something like this for the beginning:

Leader: "A story! A story!"[1]
Response: "Let it come! Let it go!"

Use something like this for the ending:

Leader: "This is the end of the story. Let everyone say AMEN."
Response: "AMEN."

There are several well-tested and unobtrusive ways to encourage audience participation: singing a hymn together, having everyone stand up to mark the beginning of the performance or to preface a prayer and then having them sit down again, or having everyone greet his/her neighbors with a hug. The performers should also thoroughly rehearse the invitations to these activities.

We like to end the rehearsal with a short prayer that helps us focus; the performance is not about us, the performers, but about those who come to watch us and listen to us. We're trying to reach

---

1. Depending on the genre, the word *story* is replaced by *letter, psalm, prophecy, vision,* and so on.

them and communicate the message of the text we're about to perform.

Here's a sample prayer:

Father in heaven,
Open our eyes, so we may see,
Open our ears, so we may hear,
And open our hearts, so we may understand.
AMEN.

Performance

At this point we have internalized the text, we have practiced gestures, we have aligned our voices to support the message of the script, and we have rehearsed; the stage has been prepared; the audience has been welcomed. Everything is in place. Now is the time to "do the text."

As soon as the performance begins, anxiety will disappear, and new dynamics will develop. The audience will stimulate the performers, time will fly, and memories will be created.

A STUDENT or teacher, scholar or clergyperson, or someone animated with simple curiosity about these ancient texts may take up the mantle of performance. A performed interpretation gives voice to what otherwise might not be heard. The performer's body lends action, movement, and visualization to what a text can only suggest, making the words, thoughts, and images come to life. When a text was performed in those early gatherings, it became (for many) a provocative, even revelatory event. In any era, performances done well can render "presence," a lived experience that is laden with levels of meaning. This alone makes them worth doing. We can think of offering a performed interpretation as a way of reverencing it and giving it the attention it deserves.

In the early Christian church, many if not most of those who would offer performances of texts were "amateurs." They wouldn't have been encouraged to try to be actors and "become" Paul or Mark or Matthew or John. They, like us, would have lent their best efforts to giving voice, personhood, understanding, empathy, and gesture to a text. As we have said throughout, some kind of competency in reading was required, and some performers might even have had formal training from Quintilian's manual. But what brought these texts to life in ways that still compel us today and invite our own efforts were the kinds of relationships our Christian forebears developed with these traditions they handed on — something in this relatively small collection of manuscripts told their stories of faith, opened up their struggles, and offered their solutions to one another.

Performing a text is a wonderful way for us to develop a relationship with it that will resonate throughout our journey of understanding.

Debriefing

"No experience is complete until it is written down," a saying goes. Likewise, the full benefit of a performance of biblical texts will be reaped only after the performance is over and the performers have had a chance to interact with each other. Often the reactions from the audience and the shared experience trigger euphoric feelings, and the group will most likely respond to each other on a very intense and deeply emotional level. The analytical work so critical for reflection is better done when there is a night between the performance and the debriefing session.

The temptation not to meet again after a performance should be resisted — especially by an academic group or by a group that's interested in encouraging spiritual growth. Often Richard and I have seen pastoral students develop critical distance and gain insights for their own practice of worship and preaching only after the performance was over; not much of this important work happened during the preparation and rehearsal of the production.

An audience might enjoy the performance, but those who presented the text will be impacted much more deeply and much longer than those who watched them. A text that presenters internalized and performed before an audience will stay with them. We speak from experience. Performed interpretations create connections between these ancient texts and lived experience; the situations described in the texts are experienced in the present.

Debriefing is a chance to express intense emotions and to put into words what was experienced. It is a time to encourage, to look forward, to be positive, and to share in a safe environment. Debriefing is not the place for devastating criticism.

A process that has worked well for us is to follow the structure of the performance and go through it section by section and performer by performer. We sit in a circle, and each performer is asked to be quiet and listen as his/her colleagues first give positive feedback, explaining what he/she did really well. Starting with a focus on positive reinforcement is based on the insight that most people find it easier to keep doing what they do well than to change bad habits.

After giving positive feedback, the group is invited to express what the performers could try to do differently if they performed that particular text again. The directors typically will hold back their opinions until everyone else has spoken.

In the second part of debriefing, we go around the circle again and ask everyone how they want to apply what they've learned. We typically discuss how we could introduce others — a class, a congregation, a Bible study group — to this way of presenting texts.

The debriefing session should end with a communal action. We like to finish meetings with a story that one of us prepared for this occasion, framed at both start and finish by the liturgical responses we developed and performed during our time together.

Conclusion

In medieval portrayals of Mary, the mother of Jesus, she is often presented as conceiving through her ear. She becomes pregnant by listening to God's message, which is conveyed to her through the voice of an angel. The image captures the experience of an ancient reader who would have received the word of God through listening. The sacred texts of faith communities promote the experience and insight that God's voice was and is heard through listening to Scripture. We have seen that, in the early days of the Christian movement, these texts were perceived as scripts to be performed before an audience.

In the Gospels, Jesus of Nazareth is presented as a storyteller. And in one of his stories, the parable of the sower, the early Christian authors have Jesus explain that the seed sown is the word. It sometimes falls on the path or on barren ground or between thorns. But, every once in a while, the word falls on fertile ground and grows. In Mark's version, Jesus performed this story on a stage — a boat — for an audience on the shore (Mark 4:1).

The author of the prologue to the Gospel according to John captured the experience that Richard and I have had over the years in the following way:

Conclusion

In the beginning was the Word. And the Word was with God.
And the Word was God. . . . And the Word became flesh and
lived among us. (John 1:1, 14)

We have seen it happen and heard participants express this
thought over and over again. When we internalize and perform
Scripture, the word comes to life and "becomes flesh" in our own
existence.

Recently, Richard and I attended a chapel service. The bulletin
had an interesting typo. When the congregation was expected to
read with their voices, instead of saying "Read responsively" the
bulletin said "Read responsibly"!

We leave you with this exhortation. It sums up what we encourage public readers of Scripture to do: to take responsibility
when it comes to the public reading of Scripture and to explore the
New Testament through performance.

Bibliography

Culture of Orality

Bauman, Richard. *Story, Performance, and Event: Contextual Studies of Oral Narrative*. Cambridge: Cambridge University Press, 1986.

Fine, Elizabeth Calvert, and Jean Haskell Speer, eds. *Performance, Culture, and Identity*. Westport, Conn.: Praeger, 1992.

Finnegan, Ruth. *Oral Poetry: Its Nature, Significance, and Social Context*. Cambridge: Cambridge University Press, 1977.

Foley, John Miles. *The Singer of Tales in Performance*. Bloomington: Indiana University Press, 1995.

—————. "The Traditional Oral Audience." *Balkan Studies* 18, no. 1 (1977): 145-53.

Fowler, Robert M. "How the Secondary Orality of the Electronic Age Can Awaken Us to the Primary Orality of Antiquity, or What Hypertext Can Teach Us about the Bible, with Reflections on the Ethical and Political Issues of the Electronic Frontier." Available online at http://www.bw.edu/~rfowler/pubs/secondoral/index.html.

Goody, Jack. *The Interface Between the Written and the Oral*. New York: Cambridge University Press, 1987.

Graham, William. *Beyond the Written Word: Oral Aspects of Scripture in the History of Religion.* Cambridge: Cambridge University Press, 1987.

Jordan, Rosan A., and Susan J. Kalčik. *Women's Folklore, Women's Culture.* Philadelphia: University of Pennsylvania Press, 1985.

Lee, Margaret Ellen, and Bernard Brandon Scott. *Sound Mapping the New Testament.* Salem, Ore.: Polebridge Press, 2009.

Niditch, Susan. *Oral World and Written Word: Ancient Israelite Literature.* Louisville: Westminster John Knox Press, 1996.

Ong, Walter J. *Orality and Literacy: The Technologizing of the Word.* London: Routledge, 1988.

——. *The Presence of the Word: Some Prolegomena for Cultural and Religious History.* Minneapolis: University of Minnesota Press, 1967.

Reinking, David. Orality and Literacy. Available online at http://www.coe.uga.edu/reading/faculty/dreinking/ONG.html.

Greco-Roman Culture of Orality

Draper, Jonathan A., ed. *Orality, Literacy, and Colonialism in Antiquity.* Atlanta: Society of Biblical Literature, 2004.

Farone, C. A. *Staging Masculinity: The Rhetoric of Performance in the Roman World.* Ann Arbor: University of Michigan Press, 2000.

Hargis, Donald. "The Rhapsode." *Quarterly Journal of Speech* 56 (1970): 388-97.

Klinghardt, Matthias. *Gemeinschaftsmahl und Mahlgemeinschaft: Soziologie und Liturgie frühchristlicher Mahlfeiern.* Tübingen: Francke, 1996.

Scobie, Alex. "Storytellers, Storytelling, and the Novel in Greco-Roman Antiquity." *Rheinisches Museum fur Philologie* 122 (1979): 229-59.

Shiner, Whitney. *Proclaiming the Gospel: First-Century Performance of Mark.* Harrisburg, Pa.: Trinity Press International, 2003.

Smith, Dennis E. *From Symposium to Eucharist: The Banquet in the Early Christian World.* Minneapolis: Fortress Press, 2003.

Taussig, Hal. *In the Beginning Was the Meal: Social Experimentation and Early Christian Identity.* Minneapolis: Fortress Press, 2009.

Orality and Literacy in Antiquity

Alexander, Loveday. "The Living Voice: Skepticism towards the Written Word in Early Christian and in Graeco-Roman Texts." In *The Bible in Three Dimensions,* ed. D. A. Clines. Sheffield: JSOT Press, 1990, pp. 221-47.

Botha, Pieter. "Greco-Roman Literacy as Setting for New Testament Writings." *Neotestamentica* 26 (1992): 195-215.

———. "Living Voice and Lifeless Letters: Reserve towards Writing in the Graeco-Roman World." *Hervormde Teologiese Studies* 49 (1993): 742-59.

———. "Mute Manuscripts: Analyzing a Neglected Aspect of Ancient Communication." *Theologia Evangelica* 23 (1990): 35-47.

Bowman, Alan K., and Greg Woolf. *Literacy and Power in the Ancient World.* Cambridge: Cambridge University Press, 1994.

Draper, Jonathan A., ed. *Orality, Literacy, and Colonialism in Antiquity.* Atlanta: Society of Biblical Literature, 2004.

Millard, A. R. *Reading and Writing in the Time of Jesus.* New York: New York University Press, 2000.

Slusser, Michael. "Reading Silently in Antiquity." *Journal of Biblical Literature* 111 (1992): 499.

Weissenrieder, Annette, and Robert B. Coote, eds. *The Interface of Orality and Writing: Speaking, Seeing, Writing in the Shaping of New Genres.* Tübingen: Mohr Siebeck, 2010.

New Testament Culture of Orality

Achtemeier, Paul. "Omni Verbum Sonat: The New Testament and the Environment of Late Western Antiquity." *Journal of Biblical Literature* 109 (1990): 3-27.

Anderson, Oivind. "Oral Tradition." In *Jesus and the Oral Gospel Tradition,* ed. Henry Wansbrough. Journal for the Study of the New Testament Supplement Series 64. Sheffield: Sheffield Academic Press, 1991, pp. 17-58.

Dewey, Joanna, and Elizabeth Struthers Malbon. *Orality and Textuality in Early Christian Literature.* Atlanta: Scholars Press, 1995.

Harvey, J. D. "Orality and Its Implications for Biblical Studies: Recapturing an Ancient Paradigm." *Neotestamentica* 30 (1996): 1-19.

Silberman, Lou H., ed. *Orality, Aurality, and Biblical Narrative.* Semeia 39. Atlanta: Scholars Press, 1987.

Classical Rhetoric

Aldrete, Gregory. *Gesture and Acclamations in Ancient Rome.* Baltimore: Johns Hopkins University Press, 1999.

Boegehold, Alan J. *When a Gesture Was Expected: A Selection of Examples from Archaic and Classical Greek Literature.* Princeton: Princeton University Press, 1999.

Bremmer, Jan, and Herman Roodenburg, eds. *A Cultural History of Gesture.* Ithaca, N.Y.: Cornell University Press, 1992.

Corbeill, Anthony. *Nature Embodied: Gesture in Ancient Rome.* Princeton: Princeton University Press, 2004.

Hall, Jon. "Cicero and Quintilian on the Oratorical Use of Hand Gestures." *Classical Quarterly* 54 (2004): 143-60.

Olbricht, Thomas. "Delivery and Memory." In *Handbook of Classical Rhetoric in the Hellenistic Period — 330 B.C. to A.D. 400,* ed. Stanley Porter. Boston, Mass.: Brill, 2001, pp. 159-67.

Shiner, Whitney. *Proclaiming the Gospel: First-Century Performance of Mark.* Harrisburg, Pa.: Trinity Press International, 2003.

New Testament Interpretation

Bailey, Kenneth. "Informal Controlled Oral Tradition and the Synoptic Gospels." *Asia Journal of Theology* 5 (1991): 34-54.

Barr, David. "The Apocalypse of John as Oral Enactment." *Interpretation* 40 (1986): 243-56.

Bechtel, Trevor. "How to Eat Your Bible: Performance and Understanding for Mennonites." *Conrad Grebel Review* 21 (2003): 81-97.

Bobertz, Charles A. "Prolegomena to a Ritual/Liturgical Reading of the Gospel of Mark." In *Reading in Christian Communities: Essays on Interpretation in the Early Church,* ed. Charles Bobertz and David Brakke. Notre Dame: University of Notre Dame Press, 2002, pp. 174-87.

Boomershine, Thomas. *Story Journey: An Invitation to the Gospel as Storytelling.* Nashville: Abingdon Press, 1988.

Botha, J. E. "Exploring Gesture and Non-Verbal Communication in the Bible and in the Ancient World: Some Initial Observations." *Neotestamentica* 30 (1996): 253-66.

Botha, Pieter. "Letter Writing and Oral Communication in Antiquity: Suggested Implications for the Interpretation of Paul's Letter to the Galatians." *Scriptura* 42 (1992): 17-34.

———. "Mark's Story as Oral Traditional Literature: Rethinking the Transmission of Some Traditions about Jesus." *Hervormde Teologiese Studies* 47 (1991): 304-31.

———. "The Verbal Art of the Pauline Letters: Rhetoric, Performance, and Presence." In *Rhetoric and the New Testament: Essays from the 1992 Heidelberg Conference,* ed. Stanley Porter and T. H. Olbricht. Sheffield: Sheffield Academic Press, 1993, pp. 409-28.

Crafton, Jeffrey. *The Agency of the Apostle: A Dramatistic Analysis of*

Paul's Responses to Conflict in 2 Corinthians. JSNTSS 51. Sheffield: Sheffield Academic Press, 1991.

Davis, Casey. *Oral Biblical Criticism: The Influence of the Principles of Orality on the Literary Structures of Paul's Epistle to the Philippians.* JSNTSS 172. Sheffield: Sheffield Academic Press, 1999.

Dewey, Joanna. "From Oral Stories to Written Texts." In *Women's Sacred Scriptures,* ed. Kwok Pui-Lon, Elisabeth Schüssler Fiorenza, and Lisa Cahill. London: SCM Press, 1998.

————. "From Storytelling to Written Text: The Loss of Early Christian Women's Voices." *Biblical Theology Bulletin* 26 (1996): 71-78.

————. "The Gospel of Mark as an Oral-Aural Event: Implications for Interpretation." In *The New Literary Criticism and the New Testament,* ed. Elizabeth Struthers Malbon and Edgar V. McKnight. Sheffield: Sheffield Academic Press, 1994, pp. 145-61.

————. "Mark as Interwoven Tapestry: Forecasts and Echoes for a Listening Audience." *Catholic Biblical Quarterly* 53 (1991): 221-31.

————. "Mark as Oral Narrative: Structures as Clues to Understanding." *Sewanee Theological Review* 36 (1992): 45-56.

————. "Oral Methods of Structuring Narrative in Mark." *Interpretation* 43 (1989): 32-44.

————. "Textuality in Oral Culture: A Survey of the Pauline Traditions." *Semeia* 65 (1995): 37-65.

Dewey, Joanna, and Elizabeth Struthers Malbon, eds. *Orality and Textuality in Early Christian Literature. Semeia* 65. Atlanta: Scholars Press, 1995.

Downing, F. G. *Doing Things with Words in the First Christian Century.* Sheffield: Sheffield Academic Press, 2000.

Dudrey, Russ. "1 John and the Public Reading of Scripture." *Stone-Campbell Journal* 6 (2003): 235-55.

Dunn, James. "Jesus in Oral Memory: The Initial Stages of the Jesus Tradition." *Society of Biblical Literature 2000: Seminar Papers.* Atlanta: Scholars Press, pp. 287-326.

Hall, Mark. "The Living Word: An Auditory Interpretation of Scripture." *Listening* 21 (1986): 25-42.

Harvey, John D. *Listening to the Text: Oral Patterning in Paul's Letters.* Grand Rapids: Baker Books, 1998.

————. "Orality and Its Implications for Biblical Studies: Recapturing an Ancient Paradigm." *Journal for the Evangelical Theological Society* 45 (2002): 99-109.

Hearon, Holly E. "The Implications of 'Orality' for Studies of the Biblical Text." Paper presented at "Orality, Narrativity, Memory: A Tribute to the Scholarship of Werner Kelber." Annual meeting of the Society of Biblical Literature, 2003.

Kelber, Werner. "Biblical Hermeneutics and the Ancient Art of Communication: A Response." *Semeia* 39 (1987): 97-105.

————. *The Oral and the Written Gospel: The Hermeneutics of Speaking and Writing in the Synoptic Tradition, Mark, Paul, and Q.* Philadelphia: Fortress Press, 1983.

Knowles, Michael. "Reading Matthew: The Gospel as Oral Performance." In *Reading the Gospels Today,* ed. Stanley E. Porter. Grand Rapids: Wm. B. Eerdmans, 2004, pp. 56-77.

McGuire, Martin. "Letters and Letter Carriers in Antiquity." *Classical World* 53 (1960): 148-53, 184-85, 199-200.

Miller, J. H. "Parable and Performative in the Gospels and in Modern Literature." In D. Jobling et al., *The Postmodern Bible Reader.* Oxford: Blackwell, 2001.

Mitchell, Margaret. "New Testament Envoys in the Context of Greco-Roman Diplomatic and Epistolary Conventions: The Example of Timothy and Titus." *Journal of Biblical Literature* 111 (1992): 641-62.

Pilch, J. J. "Actions Speak Louder than Words." *Bible Today* 34 (1996): 172-76.

Porter, Stanley E., ed. *Reading the Gospels Today.* Grand Rapids: Wm. B. Eerdmans, 2004.

Rhoads, David. "Performing the Gospel of Mark." In *Body and Bible: Interpreting and Experiencing Biblical Narratives,* ed. Björn Krondorfer. Philadelphia: Trinity Press International, 1992, pp. 102-19. Reprinted in David Rhoads, *Reading Mark, Engaging the Gospel.* Minneapolis: Fortress Press, 2004, pp. 176-201.

Scott, Bernard Brandon. *Hear Then the Parable: A Commentary on the Parables of Jesus.* Minneapolis: Fortress Press, 1990.

————. *Hollywood Dreams and Biblical Stories.* Minneapolis: Fortress Press, 1994.

————. *The Word of God in Words: Reading and Preaching the Gospels.* Fortress Resources for Preaching. Philadelphia: Fortress Press, 1985.

Shiner, Whitney. "Applause and Applause Lines in the Gospel of Mark." In *Rhetorics and Hermeneutics: Wilhelm Wuellner and His Influence,* ed. James D. Hester and J. David Hester. New York: T&T Clark International, 2004.

————. "Creating the Kingdom: The Performance of Mark as Revelatory Event." In *Literary Encounters with the Reign of God.* Festschrift for Robert Tannehill. Ed. Sharon Ringe and H. C. Paul Kim. Harrisburg, Pa.: T&T Clark International, 2004.

————. "Creating Plot in Episodic Narratives: Life of Aesop and the Gospel of Mark." In *Ancient Fiction and Early Christian Narrative,* ed. Ronald Hock, Bradley Chance, and Judith Perkins. Society of Biblical Literature Symposium Series 6. Atlanta: Scholars Press, 1998, pp. 155-76.

————. *Proclaiming the Gospel: First-Century Performance of Mark.* Harrisburg, Pa.: Trinity Press International, 2003.

Stein, R. H. "Is Our Reading the Bible the Same as the Original Audience's Hearing of It? A Case Study in the Gospel of Mark." *Journal for the Evangelical Theological Society* 46 (2003): 63-78.

Trobisch, David. "Performance Criticism as an Exegetical Method: A Story, Three Insights, and Two Jokes." In *The Interface of Orality and Writing: Speaking, Seeing, Writing in the Shaping of New Genres,* ed. Annette Weissenrieder and Robert B. Coote. Tübingen: Mohr Siebeck, 2010.

Ward, Richard. "Paul and the Politics of Performance at Corinth: A Study of 2 Corinthians 10–13." Ph.D. dissertation, Northwestern University, 1987.

———. "Pauline Voice and Presence as Strategic Communication." *Semeia* 65 (1994): 95-107.

Wire, Antoinette. "Performance, Politics, and Power: A Response." *Semeia* 65 (1994): 129-35.

Theatre

Doan, W., and T. Giles. "Masking God — Application of Drama Theory to Biblical Texts." In *Proceedings: Eastern Great Lakes and Midwest Bible Societies,* vol. 22, ed. B. Fiore. Buffalo: EGLMBS, 2002.

Erlenwein, Peter. "Bibliodrama: A Modern Body-Mind Hermeneutics." *Asia Journal of Theology* 16 (2002): 327-40.

Hecht, Anneliese. "Bibliodrama and Exegesis." *Dei Verbum* 66/67 (2003): 6-10.

Krondorfer, Björn. *Body and Bible: Interpreting and Experiencing Biblical Narratives.* Harrisburg, Pa.: Trinity Press International, 1992.

Swanson, Richard. *Provoking the Gospel: Methods to Embody Biblical Storytelling.* Cleveland: Pilgrim Press, 2004.

Speech Act Theory

Briggs, Richard. "Getting Involved: Speech Acts and Biblical Interpretation." *Anvil* 20 (2003): 25-34.

———. "The Uses of Speech Act Theory in Biblical Interpretation." *Current Research in Biblical Studies* 9 (2001): 229-76.

———. *Words in Action: Speech Act Theory and Biblical Interpretation: Toward a Hermeneutic of Self-Involvement.* Edinburgh: T&T Clark, 2001.